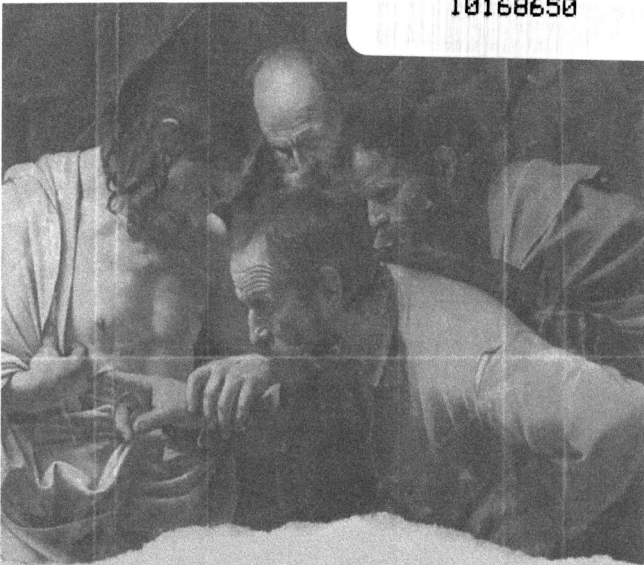

MIRACLES

What Does the Bible Really Teach?

EDWARD D. ANDREWS

MIRACLES

What Does the Bible Really Teach?

Edward D. Andrews

Christian Publishing House

Cambridge, Ohio

CHRISTIAN
PUBLISHING
HOUSE

FOUNDED 2005

MIRACLES: What Does the Bible Really Teach? by Edward D. Andrews

ISBN-10: 1949586863

ISBN-13: 978-1949586862

Table of Contents

Book Description

In an age where the existence of the supernatural is often questioned, "MIRACLES: What Does the Bible Really Teach?" emerges as a comprehensive guide exploring the enigmatic world of biblical miracles. This meticulously researched work invites readers on a journey through scriptural accounts, presenting a rigorous examination of the nature, purpose, and reality of miracles as depicted in the Holy Scriptures.

Through its in-depth analysis, the book confronts the skepticism of the modern era, dismantling naturalistic explanations and affirming the credibility of the miraculous. It delves into the laws of nature, scrutinizing their relationship with reported supernatural events, and provides a potent argument for the harmony between scientific understanding and biblical miracles.

"Understanding the Miracles of the Bible," the opening chapter, sets the stage by addressing the compatibility of miracles with natural law and God's moral framework. "The Miracles—Did They Really Happen?" progresses the discourse by examining the authenticity of these events, with a special focus on the Resurrection of Jesus Christ.

The contrast between naturalism and supernaturalism is critically explored, assessing worldviews and their implications on the interpretation of miracles. The narrative further challenges naturalistic ideologies, suggesting that such perspectives struggle to adequately explain the miraculous phenomena described within the pages of the Bible.

"Nature and Supernature" acknowledges the defined domains while showcasing instances where nature yields to divine intervention. The subsequent chapters present a compelling argument for the possibility of miracles, countering common objections and misconceptions with scholarly insight and theological acuity.

In a bold and intriguing exposition, "Unveiling Biblical Clues: The Secret Behind the Egyptian Pyramids' Creation" ventures beyond traditional discussions, examining historical enigmas through a biblical lens. "The Bible and Science" bridges faith and rational inquiry, engaging with topics like the Flood, human longevity, and the perceived scientific errors in the Bible.

The penultimate chapter, "Is Genesis' Creation of the World a Myth and Legend?" investigates the origins of the universe as presented in Genesis, juxtaposing biblical accounts with ancient creation stories.

Finally, "The Continuation of the Spiritual Gifts?" addresses the cessation of miracles, contending that while miracles served a definitive purpose during biblical times, their primary function as signs of divine endorsement concluded with the close of the apostolic age.

With rigorous scholarship and thought-provoking analysis, "MIRACLES: What Does the Bible Really Teach?" stands as an essential resource for those seeking to understand the intersection of faith, history, and the supernatural. It is an invitation to explore the biblical testimony on miracles and discover their enduring message for the contemporary world.

Preface

To our esteemed readers embarking upon this exploration of biblical miracles, welcome.

This book, "MIRACLES: What Does the Bible Really Teach?" is not merely an academic treatise; it is a quest for understanding, a journey into the heart of the miraculous as chronicled in the Scriptures. The inception of this work arose from a profound necessity to address the plethora of misconceptions and to clarify what the Bible truly conveys about the supernatural acts attributed to divine power.

In the chapters that follow, you will not find a narrative that conforms to the sensationalized portrayal of miracles common in contemporary culture. Instead, the book rigorously adheres to a faithful examination of Scripture, coupled with a respect for historical context and linguistic precision. This preface serves to align our hearts and minds with the earnest endeavor of discerning the truth amidst a sea of doubt and misrepresentation.

While the book description has acquainted you with the thematic structure and scope of this work, I invite you to approach each chapter with both an open mind and a critical eye. The discourse will bridge the expanse between ancient texts and modern understanding, challenging both skeptics and believers to reevaluate their stance on the phenomena deemed miraculous.

It is my intent to offer more than mere scholarship; this book is crafted to be a companion in your spiritual and intellectual growth. As you turn each page, may you find the content within to be a robust foundation upon which to construct or fortify your understanding of God's interactions with humanity through miraculous means.

With every word penned, my anticipation grows that you, dear reader, will encounter the miraculous not as an abstract concept, but as a tangible element of your faith narrative, rooted in the fertile ground of Scripture and watered by the quest for truth.

Thank you for joining me on this expedition through the awe-inspiring and oft-misunderstood realm of biblical miracles. Let us begin.

Edward D. Andrews

Author of 220+ books and Chief Translator of the Updated American Standard Version

Introduction

In the pages that follow, we embark on a voyage back through time and scripture, to uncover and understand the multifaceted phenomenon of miracles as portrayed in the Holy Scriptures. "MIRACLES: What Does the Bible Really Teach?" is more than a title; it is a question, a challenge, and a mission statement, rolled into one compelling inquiry that has puzzled theologians, scientists, and historians alike for centuries.

Why does the subject of miracles elicit such profound intrigue and, at times, polarizing debate? The answer lies at the intersection of our desire for the divine and our experience of the natural world. Miracles, by their very definition, suggest an intervention into natural law, a suspension of the rules governing our physical reality that we are yet to fully comprehend.

In this book, we do not shy away from the complexity that miracles present. Instead, we delve into the historical accounts, the linguistic subtleties, and the theological implications of these extraordinary events. We scrutinize the biblical text, not through the lens of modern skepticism nor with a naive acceptance, but with a scholarly rigor that honors the text and the transcendent.

The introduction serves as your guidepost, setting the stage for the in-depth discussions that will ensue. Here, we lay the groundwork for our investigation into the biblical understanding of miracles. We will consider the cultural, historical, and philosophical contexts in which these events were recorded, as well as their enduring impact on the Christian faith and worldview.

As we navigate through this investigation, we will be confronted with questions that strike at the core of belief and reason. What does it mean for an event to be considered a miracle? How do miracles relate to God's character and purpose? And perhaps most controversially, did these extraordinary events cease with the close of the scriptural canon, or do they persist in the modern era?

It is my sincere hope that this book serves as a catalyst for deeper reflection and enlightened conversation. Whether you are a steadfast believer, a curious skeptic, or somewhere in between, the exploration of miracles presented here aims to illuminate, challenge, and inspire.

So, let us begin our journey through time, text, and testimony to unravel the biblical portrayal of the miraculous. May our minds be open, our hearts receptive, and our spirits attuned to the whispers of the ages as we seek answers to one of humanity's most enduring questions: What does the Bible really teach about miracles?

CHAPTER 1 Understanding the Miracles of the Bible

Occurrences that spark amazement and astonishment are termed as miracles. These are events in the natural world that defy all recognized capabilities of humans or nature, suggesting they stem from a divine power. The term used in the Hebrew Scriptures is *moh·pheth'*, which can be translated as "miracle," but also encompasses meanings like "portent," "wonder," and "token" (Deuteronomy 28:46; 1 Chronicles 16:12). This term is frequently coupled with the word *'ohth*, which means "sign" (Deuteronomy 4:34). In the Greek Scriptures, the word *dy'na·mis*, meaning "power," is often used to signify miracles, translated into English as "ability," or "miracle" (Matthew 25:15; Luke 6:19; 1 Corinthians 12:10 in various translations).

A miracle, from the perspective of those witnessing it, is an extraordinary event that surpasses their capacity to execute or fully comprehend. It represents an act that requires a power or knowledge beyond human possession. However, to the entity that wields such power, it's not considered a miracle. The entity understands and possesses the means to perform such acts. Thus, to humans, many deeds of Jehovah appear miraculous, yet they are simply manifestations of His divine abilities. If one accepts the existence of a deity, especially Jehovah as the Creator, then acknowledging His ability to perform feats that leave humans in awe is a consistent stance (Romans 1:20).

Compatibility of Miracles with Natural Law

In the exploration of the universe, scientists have observed consistent patterns of behavior across natural phenomena, giving rise to the formulation of natural laws, such as the law of gravity. These laws, recognized for their complexity and reliability, suggest an orderly system that implies the hand of a Lawgiver. Skeptics often argue against miracles, seeing them as breaches of these natural laws, which they consider absolute and unchangeable. They contend that a true miracle is unfeasible if it cannot be reconciled with the laws as they understand them.

Yet, the stance of the scientific community on impossibilities has evolved. The renowned *Professor John R. Brobeck* highlighted that a scientist can no longer categorically declare the impossibility of an event but rather its improbability based on current knowledge. Science recognizes that it has not unraveled all mysteries of matter and energy, leaving room for phenomena, or miracles, driven by forces or sources of energy beyond our current understanding. These would be, according to our Scriptures, acts empowered by Jehovah.

The realm of scientific knowledge is constantly expanding, yet it is still far from exhaustive. Phenomena like heat, light, and atomic reactions remain not fully understood, especially under extreme conditions. For instance, investigations into supercold environments have revealed baffling behaviors in elements. Lead, usually not an ideal electrical conductor, turns into a superconductor and a powerful electromagnet when subjected to temperatures near absolute zero. Similarly, helium defies expectations by seeming to act against gravitational pull. These findings, which confound prior scientific assumptions, underscore the limited scope of human understanding.

Given these insights, how can one confidently claim that Jehovah violated His own laws when performing works that appeared miraculous to people? The Creator, who set the physical laws into motion, undoubtedly has full mastery over His creation, capable of directing natural forces in ways that align with the established order (Job 38). He could orchestrate conditions, accelerate or decelerate processes, or manipulate reactions to fulfill His purposes, sometimes through angelic agents (Exodus 3:2; Psalm 78:44-49).

Scientists themselves manipulate conditions such as temperature or chemical concentrations to achieve desired reactions without overstepping physical laws. Similarly, skeptics challenge biblical miracles, including the act of creation, presuming an exhaustive understanding of all conditions and processes throughout history. They mistakenly constrain Jehovah's capabilities within the narrow confines of human comprehension.

This intellectual limitation is not lost on the scientific community. A Swedish professor of plasma physics remarked on the difficulties of applying known laws to complex atmospheric phenomena. Just as the established laws of physics enable men to accomplish great feats, Jehovah could utilize these laws to produce outcomes that defy human expectations, such as parting the Red Sea (Exodus 14:22) or enabling a man to walk on water. The same Jehovah who stretched out the heavens has the power to intervene in His creation in ways that are unimaginable to us (Isaiah 40:21, 22, 25, 26).

Acknowledging the existence of natural laws, like gravity, inherently acknowledges a lawmaker of immense intelligence and power. Questioning His capacity to perform wonders is to inappropriately limit His operations to the scope of human knowledge and experience. The biblical character Job speaks of the folly of those who oppose their limited wisdom to that of Jehovah (Job 12:16-25; compare Romans 1:18-23).

In sum, miracles do not contravene natural law but are a testament to the supreme authority and sovereignty of Jehovah over His creation. They are a demonstration of His ability to employ the laws of the physical world in extraordinary ways, serving as signs and portents that underscore His ultimate power and purpose. This power is not confined by our limited understanding or the current scope of scientific knowledge, but it is in harmony with the complex and marvelous workings of the universe He designed and governs.

God's Adherence to His Moral Law

The God of creation is not a capricious deity who arbitrarily disregards the very laws He established. This unchanging nature of God is emphasized in the Bible: "For I the Lord do not change" (Malachi 3:6). His consistency extends to both moral and physical laws, with the former being superior in grandeur. It's clear that He upholds his moral laws with unwavering justice, refusing to condone unrighteousness. As the prophet Habakkuk affirms, "You are too pure in eyes to see what is bad; and to look on trouble you are not able" (Habakkuk 1:13).

Moral Laws and Justice

God's moral laws are a reflection of His righteousness and holiness. An illustration of His commitment to these moral principles can be seen in the principle of "an eye for an eye, a tooth for a tooth, a hand for a hand, and a foot for a foot" (Exodus 34:7; Deuteronomy 19:21). These laws ensure fairness and justice, demonstrating God's aversion to unrighteousness.

However, God's desire is not to condemn but to provide a way for repentant and helpless humans to find forgiveness and salvation. In light of this, a legal basis was required to maintain His adherence to His moral law while extending mercy to humanity. The Bible explains that sin, which leads to death, entered the world through Adam's disobedience (Romans 5:12). To remain just and righteous in forgiving those who sought His mercy, God made the ultimate sacrifice: His only-begotten Son, Jesus Christ, became the ransom for the sins of mankind.

The Sacrifice of Jesus

This profound act demonstrates the extent to which God adheres to His moral laws. He did not compromise or bend the rules but rather fulfilled them perfectly. The apostle Paul highlights this in his writings, noting that "through the release by the ransom paid by Christ Jesus," Jehovah was able to "exhibit his own righteousness . . . that he might be righteous even when declaring righteous the man that has faith in Jesus" (Romans 3:24, 26).

Consistency in Adherence to Laws

The sacrifice of Jesus Christ underscores God's unswerving commitment to His moral laws. He went to great lengths to ensure that His justice was upheld while offering a path to redemption for those who believed in Jesus. This profound sacrifice demonstrates that God's adherence to His moral laws is not arbitrary; it's a matter of divine principle, justice, and righteousness.

Adherence to Physical Laws

Given this unwavering commitment to moral laws, we can reasonably conclude that God's adherence to His physical laws is equally steadfast. The distinction between moral and physical laws is that moral laws deal with matters of righteousness and justice, while physical laws govern the operation of the physical universe.

God's integrity and consistency mean that He does not need to "violate" His own physical laws to accomplish His desires within the physical realm. In the same way that He adhered to His moral laws in providing salvation through the sacrifice of Jesus, He respects and works within the framework of His physical laws when interacting with His creation.

God's character is one of unwavering consistency and adherence to His own laws, whether they are moral or physical. His commitment to righteousness and justice is seen in His willingness to provide a legal basis for the forgiveness of human sin through the ultimate sacrifice of His Son. This sacrifice demonstrates that He can act within the framework of His moral laws while extending mercy to humanity.

In the same vein, God's respect for His physical laws is evident in the ordered and predictable nature of the universe. There is no need for Him to "violate" His physical laws to accomplish His purposes within the physical creation. Just as He upholds His moral laws with justice, so does He maintain His physical laws with the same unwavering commitment, ensuring the orderly functioning of His creation.

Contrary to Human Experience? Debunking Miracles

The challenge of accepting miracles often arises from the notion that such events seem contrary to human experience, a perspective rooted in the belief that observable phenomena, recorded history, and common human knowledge dictate what is possible. To dismiss miracles as mere superstition or myths is a significant assertion, but it is important to consider whether this skepticism holds up under scrutiny.

Challenging Historical Events

It is common for individuals living in the present day to question the truthfulness of events recorded in history, particularly those involving extraordinary occurrences like miracles. The absence of living eyewitnesses to corroborate such events may lead some to cast doubt on their authenticity. However, the fact that current observers did not experience these events does not negate their historical accuracy. It is essential to approach this challenge with a critical perspective, acknowledging that the truth of an event is not contingent upon personal experience but on reliable historical accounts.

Contradicting Human Experience

Skeptics often argue that miracles are contrary to human experience, basing their judgment on what they accept as facts derived from observation, documented history, and collective human knowledge. This perspective essentially asserts that any occurrence beyond the realm of human understanding or conventional wisdom is automatically dismissed as implausible. But this line of reasoning is not as solid as it may initially appear.

The Role of Science and Progress

If scientists were to adopt this strict stance in their work, they would curtail their research efforts significantly. Exploration, innovation, and the development of new technologies often involve the pursuit of outcomes that were once considered contrary to human experience. Scientists constantly strive to push the boundaries of what is known and understood. For instance, the quest to cure "incurable" diseases or to explore space beyond our planet exemplifies the willingness to challenge the limitations of human experience.

In this context, it is evident that human experience is not static but continues to evolve as scientific discoveries and advancements expand our understanding of the world. Modern achievements that are commonplace today would be considered miraculous by individuals from ancient times. This perspective highlights the need to remain open to the possibility of events that transcend conventional human experience.

Not "Explained Away" by Logic

Some critics of biblical miracles suggest that these extraordinary events can be rationalized and attributed to natural occurrences, dismissing them as mere products of coincidence or happenstance. While it is true that natural phenomena, such as earthquakes, were involved in some biblical narratives (1 Samuel 14:15, 16; Matthew 27:51), it is a leap to assert that these events can be solely explained through science and logic.

Timing and Unlikelihood

Many biblical miracles are characterized not only by their inherent power but also by their impeccable timing. It is the timing that often defies statistical probability and common occurrences. Take, for example, the provision of manna for the Israelites in the desert. Some have suggested that a sweet, sticky exudation found on tamarisk trees and bushes could be the basis for the manna mentioned in the Bible. Even if we were to accept this premise, the timing of the manna's appearance and behavior sets it apart as a miracle.

For instance, it did not appear on the ground on the seventh day of each week (Exodus 16:4, 5, 25-27). Additionally, the manna behaved uniquely; it bred worms and spoiled when kept beyond a day, except on the Sabbath, when it remained fresh (Exodus 16:20, 24). The description of the manna as an exudation from trees does not entirely align with the biblical account, where it is found on the ground and can undergo various preparations (Exodus 16:19-23; Numbers 11:8).

These aspects make it clear that the manna, even if it had a natural counterpart, still transcended the laws of nature in terms of its precise timing and distinct behavior. It is the extraordinary nature of these events, guided by divine orchestration, that separates them from ordinary occurrences.

Conclusion: The Balance Between Faith and Skepticism

In considering biblical miracles, it is crucial to strike a balance between faith and skepticism. While human experience and knowledge have their place in assessing the validity of extraordinary events, it is equally important to acknowledge the potential for divine intervention that defies conventional understanding. Historical accounts and narratives often challenge our preconceived notions and compel us to explore the boundaries of possibility. Miracles, as recorded in the Bible and other historical sources, provide a platform for this exploration, serving as a testament to the mysterious and awe-inspiring aspects of the world that extend beyond our ordinary experiences.

The Credibility of the Testimony of Miracles

The miraculous stands as a pillar in the foundation of Christian faith, particularly in the resurrection of Jesus Christ. This central event is supported by an array of testimonies and experiences that lend credibility to its historicity and spiritual significance. Understanding the credibility of these miracles involves examining the evidence, the character of the witnesses, and the nature of the miracles themselves.

Overwhelming Eyewitness Testimony

The resurrection of Jesus Christ is not a tale backed by a solitary claim—it is an event attested by over 500 eyewitnesses, as recorded in the New Testament (1 Corinthians 15:3-8; Acts 2:32). The sheer number of witnesses presents a powerful case for the event's authenticity. Eyewitness testimony remains a critical element in both historical documentation and legal processes; hence, the accounts of these witnesses provide a robust basis for considering the resurrection as a true historical occurrence.

Motives of the Witnesses

The motives behind the claims of Christ's resurrection further reinforce their credibility. The early Christians who proclaimed the resurrection faced persecution and death, devoid of material or political gain (1 Corinthians 15:16-19). This absence of earthly reward challenges the notion that their testimony might have been fabricated for personal advantage. The willingness to endure suffering and loss for the sake of a belief is a potent testament to its sincerity.

Characteristics of Bible Miracles

The miracles documented in the Bible possess distinct characteristics that enhance their credibility:

Public and Open Nature

Biblical miracles were often public spectacles witnessed by scores—from small groups to entire nations (Exodus 14:21-31; 19:16-19; 1 Kings 17:19-24; Mark 1:29-31; Acts 9:39-41). Jesus' miracles were notably public, with no attempt to shroud them in secrecy, and they were successful regardless of the recipient's faith (Matthew 8:16; 9:35; 12:15).

Simplicity and Spontaneity

Miracles in the Bible were marked by their simplicity and spontaneity, occurring without elaborate preparations or rituals. They were often performed in response to a simple request or need, on public streets, or in commonplace settings (1 Kings 13:3-6; Luke 7:11-15; Acts 28:3-6).

Glorifying God, Not Individuals

The motive behind the miracles was not to elevate the individual performing them but to glorify Jehovah and to point to Jesus as God's sent one (John 11:1-4, 15, 40; Revelation 19:10). These acts were designed to help others and to lead them to true worship.

Variety and Scope

The variety and scope of Biblical miracles—ranging from healing incurable diseases to controlling the weather and transforming substances—speak to the power of the Creator (Matthew 8:24-27; 1 Kings 17:1-7; 18:41-45; Exodus 7:19-21; John 2:1-11; 2 Kings 5:1-14; Luke 17:11-19; John 9:1-7). It is logical to attribute such a broad influence over creation only to its Creator.

The Logical Nature of Biblical Miracles

When considering the credibility of Biblical miracles, one must ponder the logical nature of these events. The diversity of miracles—impacting both animate and inanimate objects—reflects a power that exceeds human capability. The ability to execute such a wide range of supernatural acts suggests a force that governs all aspects of the natural world, reinforcing the notion that these miracles are credible acts of the Creator.

Assessing Credibility

In assessing the credibility of Biblical miracles, it is not sufficient to focus solely on the events themselves. One must also consider the eyewitnesses, their motives, and the characteristics of the miracles. The compelling number of witnesses, the selfless motives behind their testimony, the public and straightforward nature of the miracles, and their diversity all contribute to a logical conclusion that these events are not only plausible but also indicative of divine intervention. This logical approach to understanding Biblical miracles aligns with the conservative interpretation of scripture, recognizing the consistent thread that weaves through these extraordinary accounts—a tapestry depicting the power, wisdom, and purpose of God in human history.

The Purpose of Miracles in the Early Christian Church

Miracles played a pivotal role in the early Christian Church, serving several essential purposes that helped establish the divine nature of Christianity and the authority of those who carried its message. Understanding these purposes sheds light on the significance of miracles during the formative years of the faith.

Confirmation of God's Support

One fundamental purpose of miracles was to confirm that individuals received power and support from God. These extraordinary events served as tangible evidence of divine intervention, reinforcing the belief that a person was divinely chosen. Moses' interactions with God and the miracles he performed exemplify this confirmation (Exodus 4:1-9). Similarly, people in Jesus' time recognized that his miracles demonstrated divine backing (Exodus 4:30, 31; John 9:17, 31-33).

Identification of the Promised Prophet

God had promised the coming of a prophet in the line of Moses (Deuteronomy 18:18). Jesus' miracles were instrumental in helping people identify him as the promised prophet (John 6:14). The miraculous works of Jesus were seen as a fulfillment of the divine promise, guiding the faithful to recognize him as the one sent by God.

Supporting the Emergence of Christianity

In the early days of Christianity, miracles played a vital role in tandem with the preaching of the message. They provided individuals with the assurance that God was actively involved in the transition from the previous Jewish system to the emergence of Christianity (Hebrews 2:3, 4). These miraculous events helped establish Christianity as a legitimate faith movement with divine backing.

The Transitory Nature of Miraculous Gifts

While the first-century Christian congregation benefited from miraculous gifts, these supernatural abilities were not intended to be permanent fixtures. As the apostle Paul explained, these gifts were essential during the initial stages of the Christian congregation's development but would eventually pass away (1 Corinthians 13:8-11). This transitory nature of miraculous gifts was in line with God's purpose and the changing needs of the growing Christian community.

The Early Spread of Christianity

The history of the Acts of the Apostles reveals a period of rapid expansion and growth in the Christian Church. Jehovah's spirit worked powerfully, forming congregations and establishing Christianity in various regions (Acts 4:4; Acts 13, 14, 16-19). Within a relatively short span of time, from 33 to 70 C.E., thousands of believers congregated across diverse locations, spanning from Babylon to Rome and potentially even farther west (1 Peter 5:13; Romans 1:1,

7; 15:24). The scarcity of written copies of the Scriptures during that era, limited primarily to the affluent, necessitated the dissemination of information through oral transmission. In pagan lands, there was little knowledge of the Bible or the God of the Bible, Jehovah. This oral tradition was the primary means of sharing the Christian message, and the miraculous gifts of special knowledge, wisdom, speaking in tongues, and discernment of inspired utterances played a pivotal role in this process (1 Corinthians 12:4-11, 27-31).

The Changing Landscape of Today

In contrast to the first-century Christian community, the modern world witnesses a different reality. Virtually all necessary information is available to the literate global population, supplemented by knowledgeable Christians who can guide those who may not read but are willing to listen. Bible commentaries, concordances, and encyclopedias are readily accessible to those seeking deeper understanding. In this context, the need for God to perform miraculous acts to validate His message or His servants is diminished. Even if miraculous abilities were granted today, they would not convince all, as not even all the eyewitnesses of Jesus' miracles were persuaded to accept his teachings (John 12:9-11).

A Warning of Future Miracles

However, the Bible issues a stern warning to scoffers who dismiss the possibility of miracles. It foretells the occurrence of astounding acts of God in the future, particularly in the context of the destruction of the current wicked age under the influence of Satan (2 Peter 3:1-10; Revelation chapters 18 and 19). These forthcoming miraculous events will serve as a reminder that divine intervention is an integral part of God's plan.

Miracles in Biblical Context

In conclusion, those who deny the existence of miracles often do so because they may not believe in an invisible God or Creator or perceive His inactivity in superhuman ways since creation. Nonetheless, disbelief does not negate the profound impact of miracles as recorded in the Word of God. The accounts of these miracles, along with their divine purpose and adherence to scriptural truths, instill confidence in God's care for humanity. These miracles serve as powerful reminders that God is capable of intervening in miraculous ways, healing and blessing faithful mankind in the future, as outlined in Revelation 21:4.

CHAPTER 2 The Miracles— Did They Really Happen?

When we discuss the miracles recorded in the Bible, such as the one in Nain where Jesus resurrected a young man, it's not just about whether we find the stories emotionally stirring. It's about whether these events actually took place.

Skepticism in the Modern Era

In today's scientifically advanced age, miracles often clash with a naturalistic worldview. Many think that if something can't be tested or explained by science, it can't be real. This skepticism isn't new; it echoes the sentiments of thinkers like David Hume, who questioned miracles on the basis of what he understood about the laws of nature.

Hume's Hesitation

Hume's first point suggested that miracles defy the predictable laws of nature. We depend on the consistency of these laws in our daily lives—for instance, knowing gravity will keep us grounded. His second point argued that human gullibility and a penchant for the spectacular make us susceptible to accepting false miracles. Finally, Hume observed that claims of miracles dwindle as education and scientific understanding increase.

Are Miracles Against Nature's Laws?

Hume and others argue that a miracle is, by definition, an impossibility in our universe. Yet this assertion has a circular logic: miracles can't happen because they're miraculous. It fails to take into account that our understanding of nature's laws is not complete.

The Universe's Mysteries

In contrast to Hume's perspective, modern science acknowledges that the universe holds more mysteries than certainties. Theories of multiple dimensions, black holes, and even the reversal of time challenge the notion of immutable natural laws. Stephen Hawking's insights into the origins of the universe suggest that extreme conditions can lead to the breakdown of known physical laws.

Miracles and the Almighty

If we entertain the possibility of an almighty God, as described in the Bible, it's reasonable to consider that He might have the capacity to perform acts that are beyond our comprehension and outside ordinary natural laws. Scriptures like Exodus 15:6-10 and Isaiah 40:13, 15 depict a God who is both powerful and unconstrained by human limitations.

The Resurrection as a Foundation

The entire framework of Christian belief hinges on the greatest miracle of all: the resurrection of Jesus Christ. If Jesus rose from the dead, as the New Testament accounts claim, then it sets a precedent that miracles can and do happen.

Evaluating the Evidence

To dismiss miracles out of hand is to ignore the evidence presented in historical documents, such as the Bible. The accounts of Jesus' miracles, including the resurrection at Nain, were documented by eyewitnesses and preserved with care across centuries.

Considering the Source

The Bible isn't just another ancient text; it claims to be the inspired Word of God. If this claim is true, then it bears authority on matters including the miraculous. This isn't a matter of blind faith; it's about examining the consistency and historical reliability of the biblical narrative.

Witnesses and Wonders

It's also crucial to note that the Bible's miracles often occurred in public, with multiple witnesses. The event in Nain wasn't done in a corner but at the city gate, a public place with a crowd present.

Believing in the Miracles

In the final analysis, the possibility of miracles, including those performed by Jesus, cannot be dismissed on the basis of a naturalistic worldview alone. If one allows for the existence of God, then miracles are not just possible; they are expected manifestations of His power. The accounts of Jesus' life and the testimony of His miracles invite us to consider the reality of the supernatural intersecting with our natural world.

What About the Fakes?

The existence of fake miracles is undeniable. Many individuals claim to possess the power to heal the sick through miraculous faith healing, and some profess to be psychic surgeons capable of extraordinary healings. These claims have been scrutinized by medical experts and skeptics, including the diligent efforts of Dr. William A. Nolan.

Dr. Nolan undertook an extensive investigation into these supposed miraculous healings. His inquiry spanned evangelical faith healers in the United States and so-called psychic surgeons in Asia. The outcome of his investigation was consistent: disappointment and fraud. In other words, Dr. Nolan found no credible evidence to support the authenticity of these claimed healings.

Does Fraud Invalidate Genuine Miracles?

However, it is essential to recognize that the presence of fraudulent miracles does not automatically negate the possibility of genuine miracles. To illustrate this, let's consider some analogous situations.

For instance, there are counterfeit banknotes in circulation, but this doesn't imply that all currency is counterfeit. Likewise, some individuals may trust quack doctors or fraudulent medical practitioners, but it doesn't suggest that the entire medical profession is fraudulent. There have been skilled artists who have successfully forged "old master" paintings, yet that doesn't mean that all paintings are forgeries. Just as these examples don't invalidate the authenticity of banknotes, the medical profession, or the art world, the existence of fraudulent miracles shouldn't lead us to dismiss the possibility of real miracles.

'Miracles Do Not Happen Now'

One argument against miracles is encapsulated in the notion that "such prodigious events never happen in our days." Essentially, the skepticism arises from a lack of personal observation. David Hume, the Scottish philosopher who formulated this objection, had never personally witnessed a miracle, so he concluded that such events couldn't occur.

This line of reasoning, however, is flawed. It is unreasonable to deny the occurrence of events simply because we haven't witnessed them. Consider the remarkable events that took place long before Hume's time:

1. **The Origin of Life:** Life began on Earth, a profound and inexplicable occurrence. Certain life forms gained consciousness, and eventually, humans emerged with wisdom, imagination, the capacity to love, and a conscience. Modern science cannot fully explain these extraordinary developments based on current laws of nature, yet we exist as living evidence that they did happen.

2. **Technological Advancements:** In the centuries following Hume's era, the world has witnessed "prodigious events" driven by human innovation and scientific progress. Imagine informing Hume about contemporary marvels:

   - Communication: A businessman in Hamburg can converse with someone thousands of miles away in Tokyo without raising his voice.

- Global Broadcasting: A soccer match in Spain can be watched by people all over the world in real-time.

- Aviation: Enormous aircraft, far larger than the ocean-going ships Hume knew, can take off from the Earth's surface and carry hundreds of passengers across vast distances in just hours.

Consider Hume's possible response: "Impossible! Such prodigious events never happen in our days!"

Science and Miracles

These contemporary "prodigies" do indeed occur in our time because humanity, through the application of scientific principles that Hume could not have fathomed, has achieved these remarkable feats. We've constructed telephones, developed television sets, and invented airplanes. These achievements stand as a testament to the potential of human knowledge and ingenuity.

So, in light of these technological advancements, is it truly implausible to believe that in times long past, God, operating in ways that still elude our complete understanding, could have brought about miraculous events that defy our natural explanations? The answer is no. The presence of fake miracles and the lack of personal observation should not lead us to reject the possibility of genuine miracles, especially considering the limitless power of the divine.

How Can We Know?

As we ponder the possibility of miracles in Bible times, it's essential to acknowledge that simply acknowledging their potential existence doesn't confirm that they indeed transpired. In this 21st century, the challenge is to determine whether, in ancient times, God performed genuine miracles through His earthly servants. What sort of evidence can we reasonably expect for these extraordinary events? To grasp this, let's consider a scenario.

The Primitive Tribesman's Dilemma

Picture a primitive tribesman who, after dwelling in his jungle homeland, embarks on a journey to a vast and bustling city. He encounters the marvels of urban life but lacks the knowledge to comprehend the inner workings of an automobile or the technology behind a portable radio. He cannot construct a computer to demonstrate its existence. All he can do is share what he has witnessed.

In this regard, we find ourselves akin to that tribesman's companions. If genuine miracles transpired in the past through God's intervention, the only way to glean insight into these occurrences is by relying on eyewitness accounts. These witnesses may not possess the capability to elucidate the mechanics of these miracles or replicate them. Their role is to convey what they observed. Yet, we confront a significant challenge - eyewitnesses can be deceived, exaggerate, or inadvertently misinform.

Evaluating Eyewitness Testimony

To trust the testimony of these witnesses, we must ascertain that they are credible, of high moral character, and possess honorable motives. In essence, we require assurance that they are reliable sources of information.

The Value of Eyewitness Accounts

Eyewitness accounts carry great weight in any historical or factual analysis. In the legal system, eyewitness testimony is often considered vital in establishing the truth of an event. It's akin to pieces of a puzzle that, when properly assembled, form a coherent picture of what transpired. In the case of miracles in Bible times, eyewitnesses serve as our conduits to these remarkable occurrences.

Challenges with Eyewitness Testimony

However, relying solely on eyewitness testimony is not without its challenges. Human perception and memory can be fallible. Witness accounts may vary due to differing viewpoints or the passage of time. Moreover, eyewitnesses can be swayed by personal biases or external pressures.

The Importance of Truthfulness

To address these concerns, the veracity of the eyewitnesses is of utmost importance. If they are known to be truthful individuals, their accounts carry more weight. Truthfulness is a character trait that reflects their commitment to honesty and accuracy. It's crucial to assess whether they have a history of reliability in their statements.

Character and Morality

The moral character of the eyewitnesses is also a key factor. High moral character indicates that they possess integrity and ethical values. People with sound moral character are less likely to exaggerate or fabricate stories. Their moral conduct aligns with the principles of truthfulness and honesty.

Motive and Intent

Understanding the motives of the eyewitnesses is another aspect that we should investigate. A person's motives can significantly influence their testimony. If the witnesses have clear, honorable motives and nothing to gain from presenting false information, their credibility is enhanced.

Corroborating Evidence

While eyewitness testimony is valuable, it's even more compelling when supported by corroborating evidence. Corroboration strengthens the case for the occurrence of a miracle. This can include accounts from multiple witnesses, artifacts, or other historical records that align with the testimony.

The Uniqueness of Miracles

Miracles, by their very nature, are unique and transcend the ordinary laws of nature. They are exceptional events that defy scientific explanation. As a result, they may not be replicable or explained in human terms. This inherent uniqueness challenges the scientific method's typical requirements of repeatability and predictability.

Faith and Certainty

In the realm of miracles, faith plays a vital role. While evidence, eyewitness accounts, and corroborating information are crucial, faith also plays a part in accepting the reality of miracles. Miracles often challenge the limits of human comprehension and invite individuals to have faith in the divine. Faith, in this context, is the trust in a higher power capable of working outside the bounds of the natural world.

The Challenge of Belief

In the quest to determine whether miracles in Bible times were real, we face the challenge of assessing the credibility of eyewitness testimony. It is a complex task that requires us to consider the character, morality, and motives of these witnesses. While it may not yield absolute certainty, it can lead us to a reasonable belief in the miraculous events of the past, guided by the evidence provided by those who were there to witness them.

The Best-Attested Miracle: The Resurrection of Jesus Christ

The Historical Context

The narrative of Jesus Christ's death and resurrection unfolds with a precision that aligns with historical methods. On Nisan 14, according to the Jewish calendar, which corresponds to Thursday night by our reckoning, Jesus was arrested and tried. Found guilty of blasphemy by Jewish leaders, he was brought before Pontius Pilate, who, succumbing to external pressures, sentenced him to crucifixion on the Friday of that same week (Mark 14:43-65; 15:1-39).

The Crucifixion and Burial

The Gospels record that Jesus died quickly, confirmed by a Roman soldier's spear that pierced his side. His burial took place in a new tomb, and Nisan 15 marked a sabbath of mourning and rest. However, the events that unfolded on the morning of Nisan 16—Sunday—were to change history forever. The tomb was found empty, a discovery that would lead to the widespread claim that Jesus had risen from the dead (John 19:31–20:29; Luke 24:11).

The Empty Tomb and its Implications

The empty tomb became the central focus. The absence of Jesus' body presented a critical problem for the Jewish authorities. They could not produce a body to refute the resurrection claim. Instead, they concocted a story, bribing the guards to say the disciples stole Jesus' body (Matthew 28:11-13). Justin Martyr, about a century later, affirmed that Jewish leaders had indeed spread this counterclaim, bolstering the fact that the tomb was empty and the body was unaccounted for by natural means.

Luke the Physician's Historical Rigor

Luke, a physician by trade and a historian by calling, offers a meticulous account of these events. He had access to first-hand documents and eyewitness accounts, ensuring a high degree of accuracy in his writings. Luke's qualifications as a historian have been affirmed by scholars like Sir William Ramsay and others who recognize Luke's diligence in reporting facts (Luke 1:1-3).

Eyewitness Accounts

Key to the credibility of the resurrection are the witnesses. Individuals who knew Jesus intimately, including Matthew and John, reported seeing him alive post-resurrection. Paul, not originally a follower of Jesus, also encountered the risen Christ and cited over five hundred additional witnesses, many of whom were available for questioning at the time of his writing (1 Corinthians 15:3-8).

The Sincerity of the Witnesses

The sincerity of these witnesses is critical. They preached the resurrection as the cornerstone of their faith, at great personal cost. The transformation in their lives, from hiding in fear to proclaiming the risen Christ boldly, speaks to the genuineness of their testimony (1 Corinthians 15:14, 17). Their willingness to face hardship and martyrdom reinforces the authenticity of their claims.

Miracles as Historical Reality

The resurrection stands as a substantiated historical event. This lends credibility to other biblical miracles, supported by eyewitness testimony. The same divine power that raised Jesus enabled the miracles he performed during his ministry (Luke 7:11-15; Matthew 11:4-6; 14:14-21, 23-31).

In conclusion, the best-attested miracle in the Bible, the resurrection of Jesus Christ, serves not only as a keystone of Christian faith but also as a testament to the reliability of biblical narrative and the reality of miracles. The thorough documentation of the events, the character and sincerity of the witnesses, and the corroborative external evidence point to a conclusion that aligns with historical, logical, and theological scrutiny: Jesus' resurrection on Nisan 16, 33 C.E. is a historical reality, a miracle that affirms the Bible as the true Word of God.

CHAPTER 3 The Naturalist and the Supernaturalist

Worldviews in Conflict: Naturalism vs. Supernaturalism

In the discourse between naturalism and supernaturalism, the Bible holds a definitive stance, illustrating a history steeped in divine acts that defy natural explanation. This chapter will delve into the conflicts between the naturalist and supernaturalist worldviews, assessing the biblical account of miracles and God's sovereign interventions against the backdrop of a world that often views such notions with skepticism or outright denial.

The Naturalist Perspective

Naturalism is the belief that everything arises from natural properties and causes, and supernatural explanations are not needed or are invalid. In this view, the laws of nature are consistent and unbreakable, and all phenomena can be explained by these laws or are yet to be understood within this framework. For naturalists, miracles depicted in the Bible are often seen as myths or allegories, not as literal historical events.

The Supernaturalist Standpoint

Contrastingly, supernaturalism holds that there is more to reality than can be grasped by natural laws and sciences. It acknowledges the existence of a divine realm and entities that can, and do, interact with the natural world, often in ways that are beyond our understanding or current scientific explanation. For supernaturalists, the miracles recorded in Scripture are factual events that bear witness to the power and presence of God.

The Miraculous in Biblical Accounts

Throughout the biblical text, miracles are a common thread. The Hebrew term for miracle, נֵס (*nes*), often connotes a "sign" or "banner" raised to signal the presence or intervention of God. The Greek term σημεῖον (*sēmeion*) carries the notion of a sign that indicates divine action. Both terms suggest that miracles are more than mere wonders; they are indicators pointing to Jehovah's direct involvement with His creation.

Balancing Two Realities

The crux of the conflict between naturalism and supernaturalism lies in the interpretation of events that appear to transcend natural laws. The biblical worldview presents a balance: the laws of nature are upheld as Jehovah's consistent patterns for the universe (Jeremiah 33:25), yet it also affirms that He can and does act outside these patterns when He deems it necessary.

For example, the parting of the Red Sea (Exodus 14) is portrayed not merely as a natural event but as an extraordinary act where God commanded the waters to move—a clear departure from naturalism. In the New Testament, the resurrection of Jesus (Matthew 28:1-10) stands as the foundational miracle of Christian faith, a supernatural event that naturalism cannot accommodate.

Miracles as Foundations and Witnesses

In biblical times, miracles served as foundational events that established the credibility of Jehovah's messengers and confirmed the divine origin of their message. Moses's miracles in Egypt, Elijah's contest on Mount Carmel (1 Kings 18), and Jesus's resurrection are pivotal events that defined their respective eras of biblical history.

The Role of Written Scripture

As the completed Scriptures became available, the recorded word began to serve as the primary means by which Jehovah communicates His will to humanity. Hebrews 1:1-2 expresses that God, who at various times and in different ways spoke in time past to the fathers by the prophets, has in these last days spoken to us by His Son. The implication is that the miraculous events and the gifts of the Holy Spirit that accompanied the apostles were for a time when the written New Testament was not yet available.

Miracles and Faith Today

Given the biblical perspective that the age of foundational miracles has passed, one might conclude that supernaturalism has no place in the modern Christian's worldview. However, this would be an oversimplification. The Scripture does not discount the possibility of Jehovah's intervention in response to prayer or in times of need; it simply reframes the expectation that such events should be commonplace or a basis for faith.

The Importance of Historical-Grammatical Interpretation

Adhering to the objective historical-grammatical method of interpretation, miracles in the Bible are understood within their historical context. The method requires that the biblical text be taken seriously in its historical setting, acknowledging that the supernatural interventions described were indeed extraordinary and not typical of Jehovah's usual manner of operation, which often uses natural means and respects the established order of creation.

A Worldview Rooted in Scripture

The conservative biblical scholar recognizes that the worldview of the Bible encompasses both natural laws and the reality of the supernatural, without conflating the two or dismissing either. While miracles in the biblical narrative are historical, they are not prescribed as the normative experience for believers today. The miracles of the Bible served specific purposes in salvation history and were meant to point to Jehovah and His plan for humanity. As such, the modern Christian is encouraged to live by faith in the sufficiency of Scripture and in the providence of God, who is still at work in the world, though not necessarily through overt miraculous signs.

Understanding the Naturalist Perspective on Miracles

To deeply comprehend the naturalist perspective on miracles, it's essential to engage with the premise that underpins naturalism: the unwavering belief in the constancy and exclusivity of natural laws. From this standpoint, all phenomena, without exception, are considered to be products of material causes and effects that are observable, predictable, and fundamentally scientific.

Natural Law and the Exclusion of the Divine

Naturalism posits that natural laws govern the universe, and these laws are immutable and impersonal. They do not bend, nor do they break, and thus anything that seems to violate these laws is either misunderstood or misinterpreted. The naturalist looks at the world and sees a system that operates according to these fixed rules, which can be understood and described through human observation and reason.

Miracles in the Light of Natural Law

When confronting biblical accounts of miracles, such as the תכין (*tekhin*, resurrection) of Lazarus (John 11:38-44), the naturalist approach would seek a natural explanation or dismiss the event as a legend or myth. To the naturalist, the concept of Jesus restoring life to a dead man is incompatible with the known laws governing life and death. Thus, they argue, the story must be an allegory or an embellishment by early Christians, not a factual historical event.

The Redefinition of the Miraculous

From the naturalistic view, the term "miracle" itself may be redefined. Rather than being an intervention by a supernatural deity, a miracle may be seen as an extraordinarily rare or statistically unlikely event within the bounds of natural possibility. For instance, the naturalist may regard the survival of a person in a near-fatal accident as a "miracle," not attributing the outcome to divine intervention but to a rare convergence of favorable circumstances.

Methodological Naturalism in Biblical Scholarship

In biblical scholarship, methodological naturalism insists on seeking natural explanations for events described in the biblical texts. It assumes that, even if the text claims a supernatural cause, there must be a natural cause that was perhaps beyond the understanding of the ancient writer. This approach often leads to rationalizing miracles, like the plagues of Egypt, as natural phenomena that were given a theological interpretation by the Israelites.

The Role of Probability and Evidence

Naturalists often argue that since miracles are, by definition, violations of natural laws, they are the least probable explanation for any event. Following Occam's Razor—a principle suggesting that the simplest explanation is usually the right one—naturalists assert that a natural explanation, no matter how improbable, is always more likely than a supernatural one because it doesn't require an exception to the rules that govern reality.

Critiques of the Naturalist Perspective

The naturalist perspective faces critiques for potentially dismissing firsthand experiences and historical accounts that claim supernatural elements. By prioritizing a materialistic interpretation, it may be argued that naturalism fails to account for the full range of human experience and historical documentation. Moreover, it might be viewed as limiting the possibility of divine agency, which is central to the theistic understanding of the world.

The Challenge of Miracles to Naturalism

Miracles, by their very nature, challenge the core of naturalism because they suggest that there is a force beyond nature that can intervene in the physical world. When Jesus turned water into wine at Cana (*Κανὰ τῆς Γαλιλαίας*, John 2:1-11), for example, the naturalist must either reject this as a historical event or attempt to explain it through natural causes—both options that fail to satisfy the supernaturalist's interpretation.

Historical Consideration of Miracles

In considering the historical aspect, the naturalist might concede that Jesus and other biblical figures were indeed historical and that they likely had a profound impact on their contemporaries. However, they would attribute the reports of miracles to the ancient people's lack of scientific understanding or to the writers' intent to convey theological truths rather than literal histories.

The Limits of Naturalism in Understanding Scripture

While naturalism has its place in scholarly investigation and scientific inquiry, when it comes to understanding the Bible, its principles can be too confining. The Bible itself does not present miracles as mere natural phenomena but as significant events that reveal Jehovah's character, purpose, and interaction with humanity. A naturalist reading strips these events of their intended meaning and diminishes the narrative's theological significance.

A Divided Stance on Miracles

In summary, the naturalist perspective on miracles takes a stance that is fundamentally divided from the supernaturalist view. While naturalism strives to maintain a consistent framework that excludes the need for divine intervention, the biblical accounts stand as a testament to the belief in a God who is both willing and able to perform wonders that defy human explanation. For the believer, miracles are not simply unlikely events within the natural order but are signs of Jehovah's sovereignty and testimony to His relationship with His creation.

The Supernaturalist Stance: Comprehending Biblical Intervention

In the exploration of miracles within the Christian scriptural context, the supernaturalist stance is distinct in its acknowledgment of divine intervention as a real and potent factor in the events of the world. This perspective stands in stark contrast to the naturalist view, for it allows, and indeed expects, that the divine hand of God—Jehovah—may directly influence and alter the natural order to fulfill His purposes.

Miracles as Acts of Divine Authority

Supernaturalists hold that miracles are not random or arbitrary but are demonstrations of divine authority and power, often rendered in the original texts as δύναμις (*dunamis*), which conveys the concept of strength, power, or ability inherent in God's nature. This is illustrated in accounts such as Jesus calming the storm (Mark 4:39), where His command, "Peace! Be still!" (Σιώπα, πεφίμωσο!), immediately subdued the natural elements, revealing His lordship over creation.

Divine Intervention in the Old Testament

In the Old Testament, miracles serve as direct interventions by Jehovah, affirming His sovereignty and fulfilling His covenant promises. The ten plagues on Egypt, culminating in the פֶּסַח (*pesach*, Passover) and the liberation of the Israelites, demonstrate God's power over the Egyptian deities and His deliverance of His people (Exodus 7-12). These acts are not merely symbolic gestures but are understood as historical events with theological significance, attesting to Jehovah's commitment to His chosen people.

Miracles as Fulfillment of Prophecy

Supernaturalists assert that miracles often served to authenticate the messenger of God, fulfilling ancient prophecies. For example, Isaiah's prophecy about the coming Messiah included miraculous signs (Isaiah 35:5-6). The fulfillment of this prophecy is seen in Jesus's healing of the blind and the lame, signifying His divine mission and identity as the promised Χριστός (*Christos*, Messiah).

New Testament Miracles as Divine Endorsement

In the New Testament, miracles by Jesus and the apostles are seen as divine endorsements of their message and ministry. The apostle John refers to these miracles as σημεῖα (*semeia*, signs) that reveal Jesus's glory and lead to belief (John 2:11). The supernaturalist views these not as mere myth or metaphor but as historical realities that validate the new covenant in Jesus's blood.

The Apostolic Age: A Unique Epoch for Miracles

The supernaturalist perspective contends that the apostolic age was a unique epoch in which miracles served a foundational role. This aligns with the understanding that the early Christian miracles recorded in the Acts of the Apostles were signs to establish the church and to confirm the apostolic testimony of the risen Christ. The healing of the lame man at the temple gate by Peter and John (Acts 3:1-10) is one such example, which authenticated their message and resulted in many people believing their preaching.

Miracles as Divine Communication

Furthermore, miracles are viewed as a form of divine communication, ways in which Jehovah interacted with His creation to reveal His nature, intentions, and plans. The virgin birth of Jesus (παρθένος γέννησις, Matthew 1:23), for instance, is seen as a sign of God's direct action in history, bringing about the incarnation of the divine Word (Λόγος), fulfilling prophetic scriptures, and demonstrating His ability to operate outside of natural processes.

The Historical-Grammatical Method and Miracles

The supernaturalist stance, particularly within conservative scholarship, often employs the historical-grammatical method in interpreting biblical accounts of miracles. This method seeks to understand the text by considering the historical context and the author's original intent, affirming the veracity of the miracle narratives as literal events that took place within history.

Theological Implications of Miracles

Theologically, miracles are seen as expressions of Jehovah's attributes—His omnipotence, omniscience, and omnipresence. They are actions that unveil His character and His engagement with the world. In the miraculous feeding of the 5,000 (ἀρτοκλασία), Jesus's provision pointed to Jehovah Jireh, the God who provides, while also prefiguring the spiritual nourishment offered in Christ.

Post-Apostolic Miracles: A Shift in Understanding

While recognizing the reality of biblical miracles, the supernaturalist acknowledges a shift after the apostolic age. With the establishment of the Christian canon, the nature of divine intervention shifted away from public, observable miracles to more subtle guidances of providence. This does not negate the possibility of miracles but suggests a change in their function and frequency. They argue that miracles served their purpose in authenticating the early church, and with the complete canon of Scripture, God now speaks through His written Word rather than through signs and wonders.

In sum, the supernaturalist stance comprehends miracles as divine interventions that affirm Jehovah's sovereign will, communicate His purposes, and authenticate His messengers. Miracles are not seen as contraventions of natural law but as the natural outcome of the divine nature engaging with the created order. This understanding underscores the biblical testimony of a God who is actively involved in His creation, directing history toward His ultimate redemptive purpose. The foundational role of miracles in the biblical narrative is affirmed, while also acknowledging the distinct shift in the operation and purpose of miracles in the life of the post-apostolic church.

Balancing Act: Natural Laws and Supernatural Claims

Within the annals of Judeo-Christian scriptures, the narrative of God's interaction with creation often challenges our understanding of natural laws through the assertion of supernatural claims. To the conservative scholar, these claims are not merely illustrative or allegorical but are testimonies of historical interventions by a transcendent deity, Jehovah, who is not limited by the physical laws He has ordained.

Understanding Natural Laws in Biblical Context

Natural laws are the observed regularities in nature, perceived and articulated through human investigation and reasoning. In Biblical Hebrew, the idea of a natural order is sometimes captured by words like חֻקָּה (chuqqah), implying a prescribed task or statute, and מִשְׁפָּט (mishpat), often referring to a judgment or a law. In the Greek, νόμος (nomos) carries the idea of established laws or customs. These words reflect an understanding that creation operates according to a divine order or set of parameters.

The Supernatural Overriding Natural Order

Yet, the Bible presents instances where this natural order is overridden—where δύναμις (*dunamis*), the power of God, interjects. Consider the parting of the Red Sea (יַם סוּף, Exodus 14:21-22), where the natural law of gravity and the physical properties of water were suspended. From the supernaturalist viewpoint, this was not a contravention of natural laws but a demonstration that the Creator governs and can supersede these laws.

Miracles as Enhanced Natural Phenomena

Some scholars suggest that certain Biblical miracles may be understood as an enhancement of natural phenomena. Joshua's long day (יוֹם אָרֹךְ, Joshua 10:13) might be perceived not as a halting of the earth's rotation but as a prolonging of light by refraction or other means. However, a strict supernaturalist insists that such events should be taken at face value—divine actions beyond our scientific comprehension.

Christ's Miracles and Natural Law

In the New Testament, Jesus's miracles are particularly illustrative of this balance between natural laws and supernatural claims. Turning water into wine at Cana (John 2:1-11) showcases a transformation of substance that defies chemical and physical laws. It presents the idea that Jesus, being the Λόγος (*Logos*), has authority over both the natural and the supernatural order.

The Purpose of Miracles: Signposts to Divine Truth

Miracles in the scriptures serve a dual purpose: to meet human needs and to act as signposts to divine truth. Jesus's feeding of the multitude with five loaves and two fish (μόλις ἀρτοκλασίας, Matthew 14:17-21) addresses an immediate physical need while also pointing to the greater spiritual nourishment He offers. This aligns with Jesus's own words that His miracles are works from the Father to lead people to belief (John 10:37-38).

Resurrection: The Ultimate Supernatural Claim

The resurrection of Jesus from the dead (ἀνάστασις, Matthew 28:5-6) stands as the pinnacle of supernatural claims. It is a profound event that not only violates the observable law of biogenesis but also serves as the central tenet of Christian faith. To the supernaturalist, this is an incontrovertible event that confirmed Jesus's deity and the power of God to give life.

The Prophetic Nature of Miracles

Prophets in the Old Testament performed miracles as signs of divine authentication. Elijah's calling down fire from heaven (1, אֵשׁ מִן הַשָּׁמַיִם Kings 18:38) and Elisha's purifying of the poisoned stew (2, מָרָק מָוֶת Kings 4:38-41) are such instances. These acts transcended natural laws and served as concrete evidence of their prophetic office and the truth of their message.

The Role of Faith in Understanding Miracles

Faith, or πίστις (*pistis*), plays a crucial role in the supernaturalist's understanding of miracles. While natural laws are comprehended through observation and reason, miracles require a belief in a power beyond the natural. The healing miracles of Jesus often came with an admonition to faith, as in the healing of the woman with the issue of blood (Mark 5:34), indicating that faith is the lens through which the supernatural is perceived and received.

Divine Providence and Natural Law

The supernaturalist stance holds that even within the regularity of natural laws, there is room for the divine providence of God. Jehovah's ongoing governance of the world may not always manifest through overt miracles but through what might be considered providential orchestration of natural events.

In conclusion, the supernaturalist viewpoint maintains a harmonious balance between respect for natural laws and the acknowledgement of supernatural claims as presented in the Bible. This perspective does not view miracles as anomalies or myths but as genuine acts of God that serve a purpose within His sovereign plan. They are seen as both historical events and theological revelations, pointing beyond themselves to the reality of a God who is both immanent in and transcendent over His creation.

Edward D. Andrews

CHAPTER 4 The Cardinal Difficulty of Naturalism

Identifying the Core Challenges of Naturalism

Naturalism, as a philosophical viewpoint, posits that everything arises from natural properties and causes, and supernatural or spiritual explanations are excluded or discounted. This perspective presents several challenges when interfaced with the Biblical narrative, which frequently incorporates elements that transcend natural explanation.

The Constraint of Methodological Naturalism

Methodological naturalism is a principle in scientific inquiry that assumes all phenomena have natural causes. While it is a fruitful method for scientific investigation, it inherently dismisses the possibility of supernatural intervention. For example, the Biblical account of the resurrection of Jesus (ἀνάστασις) defies the naturalistic assumption since it posits an event outside the scope of natural causes—life from death.

Naturalism and the Historical Miracles of the Bible

The Bible recounts miracles that showcase direct divine intervention, such as the plagues in Egypt (נגעים, Exodus 7-11) and the Virgin Birth (ἡ κατὰ σάρκα γέννησις τοῦ

Χριστοῦ, Matthew 1:23). Naturalism struggles with such accounts because they cannot be explained by natural causes or processes. They either have to be reinterpreted, often reducing them to mere myths or allegories, or outright denied.

The Philosophical Presuppositions of Naturalism

Naturalism carries with it certain philosophical presuppositions, primarily that the natural world is all that exists. This view is in direct contrast to the Biblical teaching of a transcendent God who is actively involved in His creation. The philosophical underpinnings of naturalism reject the possibility of miracles and divine action, which are fundamental to the Biblical narrative.

The Limitations of Naturalism in Explaining Consciousness and Morality

Naturalism faces significant difficulties in accounting for consciousness and morality. The Biblical view of humans as beings created in the image of God (צֶלֶם אֱלֹהִים, Genesis 1:27) provides a basis for the reality of free will and moral responsibility. Naturalism, on the other hand, tends to reduce human thoughts and behaviors to biochemical processes, which may negate genuine free will and moral accountability.

The Exclusivity of Naturalistic Explanations

Naturalism strictly confines itself to causes within the natural realm, but this raises questions when considering the origin of the universe itself. For example, the doctrine of creation ex nihilo (creation out of nothing, בראשית, Genesis 1:1) is irreconcilable with naturalism, which cannot adequately explain the emergence of something from nothing without an external, transcendent cause.

The Challenge of Miracles in the Lives of Saints

Throughout church history, there have been claims of miracles in the lives of saints. While naturalism would dismiss these as fabrications or misunderstandings of natural phenomena, to the believer, they are seen as confirmations of faith. The healings attributed to the apostles (ἀπόστολοι, Acts 5:12-16) would be deemed impossible under naturalistic assumptions, yet they are an integral part of the historical claims of Christianity.

"Saints" Is not Rendering

The term "saints" within the biblical context refers to those who are set apart as holy to Jehovah—those who have been called to follow Christ and are thus sanctified through their faith and obedience. When mentioning the healings attributed to the apostles, this is in reference to the early followers of Jesus Christ during the foundational period of the Christian congregation, as recorded in the Acts of the Apostles. These first-century Christians were recognized for their faithful service and commitment to the teachings of Jesus, and they were known to perform miraculous works as a testimony to the truth of the Gospel message.

The mention of miracles in the lives of these early Christians is meant to illustrate the continuity of divine action from the Old Testament, through the life of Jesus, and into the period of the early church. The New Testament describes these miraculous events not as commonplace occurrences but as significant signs that established the authority of the apostles' message and validated the new covenant in Christ's blood.

In contrast to this, the use of the term "saints" in later church history, it takes on a variety of meanings that are not consistent with the biblical usage. Some traditions revere individuals who have been officially canonized and attribute miraculous intercessions to them. However, from a biblical standpoint, all true followers of Christ are considered saints or holy ones (UASV), without the necessity of canonization or veneration of relics. These individuals are holy because of their positional standing before God through their union with Christ, not due to any inherent righteousness or miraculous works posthumously attributed to them.

In this sense, when discussing the healings by the apostles or the early Christians, the emphasis is on those within the scriptural record—particularly within the time frame of the writing of the New Testament—whose lives bore witness to the power and message of the risen Lord through the Spirit. The miraculous events associated with these individuals serve a distinct purpose in redemptive history, attesting to the veracity of the Christian faith and the hand of God actively at work among His people.

In adhering to a literal interpretation of Scripture, it's important to differentiate between the biblical definition of saints or holy ones and later developments within Christian history that may not align with the historical-grammatical context of the biblical text. The New Testament's portrayal of miracles is tied to the proclamation of the Gospel and the establishment of the early church, not as a precedent for ongoing miraculous events throughout all of church history.

The Reduction of Biblical Texts to Natural Phenomena

A naturalistic approach to the Bible may attempt to explain miraculous events as misunderstandings of natural occurrences. For instance, the parting of the Red Sea (יָם סוּף, Exodus 14:21-22) is sometimes explained as a natural event caused by wind patterns. However, such explanations often fall short of the textual descriptions that emphasize divine intervention.

The Dismissal of Prophetic Fulfillment

Prophecy is a significant aspect of the Biblical narrative, with predictions often fulfilled in extraordinary ways. Naturalism would view prophetic fulfillment as coincidence or retroactive insertion into the text. Yet, for the conservative scholar, the specific nature of prophecies, such as those concerning the Messiah (מָשִׁיחַ, Daniel 9:25-26), and their fulfillment are seen as evidence of a divine orchestration that transcends naturalistic explanation.

The Disconnection from a Historical Faith Tradition

Christian faith is historically rooted in the belief in miracles, from the Old Testament through the New Testament, into the early Church and beyond. Naturalism, by its rejection of the supernatural, severs itself from this historical faith tradition, resulting in a form of Christianity that is fundamentally different from that of the early believers.

The Ultimate Challenge: The Resurrection

The resurrection of Jesus Christ (*ἀνάστασις τοῦ Χριστοῦ*) stands as the cardinal difficulty for naturalism within Christian theology. It is the cornerstone of Christian faith (1 Corinthians 15:14-19), and a naturalistic worldview must reject it as historical fact, thereby undermining the very foundation of Christian doctrine.

Naturalism presents substantial challenges when it attempts to engage with the Biblical narrative and the Christian faith tradition. Its presuppositions are at odds with the core beliefs of Christianity, creating a tension that often leads to a reinterpretation or rejection of fundamental doctrines. For the conservative scholar, the consistent witness of Scripture, the continuity of the faith tradition, and the philosophical depth of Christian doctrine affirm a reality that includes both natural and supernatural dimensions.

The Bible's Supernatural Narrative vs. Naturalistic Explanations

The Bible's Supernatural Narrative vs. Naturalistic Explanations

The Bible presents a narrative replete with supernatural events that form the bedrock of Judeo-Christian belief. This supernatural narrative often stands in stark contrast with naturalistic explanations that seek to explain our world solely through the lens of observable and measurable phenomena.

The Miraculous Genesis of Life

The account of creation found in the book of Genesis (בְּרֵאשִׁית, Genesis 1-2) offers a vivid portrayal of divine creativity that surpasses natural processes. Naturalism insists on evolutionary mechanisms to explain the diversity of life. In contrast, the Biblical narrative describes a series of creative acts by Jehovah (יהוה) that culminate in a world teeming with life, including the special creation of humans in His image (צֶלֶם אֱלֹהִים).

Divine Intervention in Human History

The narrative of the Exodus, where Jehovah unleashes plagues upon Egypt (מַכּוֹת מִצְרַיִם, Exodus 7-11), culminating in the parting of the Red Sea (קְרִיעַת יַם־סוּף, Exodus 14:21-22), challenges naturalism directly. Naturalistic interpretations that seek to demythologize these events often fail to capture the profound sense of divine interaction that the text conveys.

The Prophetic Tradition and Predictive Miracles

Prophecies throughout the Hebrew Scriptures (תנ"ך) contain elements that defy naturalistic explanation, particularly those that predict future events with precise detail. For example, the prophecies concerning the suffering servant in Isaiah (עֶבֶד יהוה, Isaiah 53) and the specific prophecies concerning the Messiah's arrival (מָשִׁיחַ, Daniel 9:25-26) are fulfilled in the New Testament with uncanny accuracy. These are hard to reconcile within a naturalistic framework that discounts foresight in history.

The Miracles of Jesus

The New Testament is replete with accounts of Jesus' miracles (σημεῖα καὶ τέρατα, John 4:48), from healings to the control over nature, to raising the dead. Naturalism has no framework to account for these occurrences, often relegating them to the realm of allegory or myth. Yet, within the Christian tradition, these works (ἔργα, John 5:36) serve as a testament to Jesus' divine authority and the inauguration of God's Kingdom.

The Virgin Birth

The conception and birth of Jesus (γέννησις τοῦ Ἰησοῦ, Matthew 1:18-25) present a direct challenge to naturalism. The Greek term παρθένος (parthenos) clearly indicates a virgin, underscoring the supernatural nature of Jesus' birth. This event transcends naturalistic explanations and is pivotal in the Christian understanding of the incarnation of the divine Word (λόγος, John 1:1,14).

The Resurrection as the Apex of the Supernatural

The resurrection of Jesus Christ (ἀνάστασις, 1 Corinthians 15) remains the most formidable event that naturalism cannot adequately explain. The empty tomb and witnessed appearances of the risen Christ (Χριστός) defy all naturalistic explanations and serve as the cornerstone of the Christian faith.

The Ascension and Exaltation of Christ

Following His resurrection, the ascension of Jesus (*ἀνάληψις*, Acts 1:9-11) signifies His exaltation and current reign in heaven. This event, too, presents an episode that lies outside the purview of naturalism, asserting the continued Lordship of Christ (*Κύριος*) over all creation.

The Eschatological Hope

The promise of a new creation (*καινὴ κτίσις*, Revelation 21:1) where God will dwell with humanity defies naturalistic frameworks, which can only foresee an end to our universe dictated by entropy and decay. The Biblical narrative of an ultimate restoration and transformation offers a hope that is supernatural at its core.

The Power of the Holy Spirit in the Early Church

The book of Acts describes the outpouring of the Holy Spirit (*πνεῦμα ἅγιον*, Acts 2) upon the early Christian community, empowering them for ministry and witnessing through miraculous signs. This event cannot be contained within a naturalistic explanation but points to the dynamism of divine action within the historical context of the church's mission.

The Tension between Faith and Naturalism

The conservative scholar must acknowledge that the tension between the Biblical narrative and naturalistic explanations is not merely an intellectual exercise. It is a matter of faith's intersection with reason. The supernatural events of the Bible, especially miracles, are not meant to be mere footnotes in history but are presented as signals of God's involvement in the world He created. The naturalist worldview can offer no satisfactory explanation for these events, nor can it provide the existential meaning and hope that such miracles engender for believers.

The Bible's supernatural narrative provides a rich, textured understanding of reality that includes the physical and the metaphysical, the observable and the unseen. This stands in marked contrast to the naturalistic explanations that operate solely within the parameters of the material world. The miracles described in the Scriptures, therefore, are not just ancient tales but formative events that define the faith and hope of believers, beckoning beyond the boundaries of naturalism to a reality suffused with divine presence and power.

Miracles in Question: The Main Hurdle for Naturalists

In a world where empirical evidence and the scientific method are held as the benchmarks for truth, the concept of miracles presents a significant challenge to the naturalist paradigm. To a naturalist, who maintains that natural laws are unbreakable and that all phenomena must be explainable by natural causes, miracles are not just improbable; they are impossible.

The Naturalistic Framework and Miracles

Within the naturalistic framework, the universe is a closed system. All events, no matter how extraordinary, are believed to have causes that can be understood and explained within the parameters of nature's laws. This view is often rooted in a materialistic perspective that denies the existence of anything beyond the physical. Therefore, the notion that an omnipotent Being could intervene in the natural order is inconceivable to a naturalist. Miracles, by their very definition, are events that defy natural explanations. In the Bible, we see miracles as acts of Jehovah that confirm His power and purposes. They are historical events that fall outside of naturalistic explanations but are perfectly rational when one acknowledges the existence of a supernatural Creator.

Historical Claims of Miracles and Naturalistic Interpretations

The Bible is replete with accounts of miraculous events. Consider the Hebrew word for miracle, *nes* (נֵס), which often conveys a sense of a banner or a sign. These signs serve a dual purpose: they are demonstrations of Jehovah's power and also communicative acts, revealing divine truths to humanity. The New Testament Greek word *dunamis* (δύναμις), often translated as "power" or "mighty work," points to acts that exhibit the power of God.

When examining biblical miracles such as the ten plagues of Egypt (Exodus 7–12), the naturalist approach often resorts to seeking natural explanations for these events. For example, some have posited that the Nile turning to blood could have been a natural phenomenon caused by red algae. However, such explanations fall short when one considers the timing, the specificity of the plagues, and the fact that they ceased at Jehovah's command.

In the New Testament, Jesus's miracles, such as turning water into wine (John 2:1-11), healing the sick (Mark 5:25-34), and raising Lazarus from the dead (John 11:1-44), present an even greater challenge to naturalism. The immediacy and public nature of these events defy naturalistic explanations. The Greek texts underscore these acts as *semeia* (σημεῖα), signs pointing to Jesus's divine authority and identity.

The Resurrection: Naturalism's Greatest Challenge

Perhaps the most formidable biblical event that naturalism must contend with is the resurrection of Jesus Christ. The apostle Paul underscores the centrality of this miracle to the Christian faith (1 Corinthians 15:14-19). The resurrection is the linchpin of Christian doctrine, and if it could be explained away by natural causes, the entire faith would crumble. Yet, the historical evidence for the resurrection, the transformation of the apostles, and the emergence of the early church amidst persecution, attest to the fact that something extraordinary happened.

Naturalism's Limitations in Historical Analysis

Naturalism's adherence to natural causes as the only valid explanation for events imposes a limitation on the interpretation of historical phenomena. This approach can often lead to a dismissal of historical testimony and documents, such as the biblical accounts, if they include elements that transcend naturalistic boundaries. However, such dismissiveness can be seen as a methodological bias rather than a neutral stance. To fully engage with the biblical accounts of miracles, one must consider the possibility of the supernatural, which is an integral part of the historical and cultural context of the texts.

The main hurdle for naturalists when facing miracles is not the lack of historical evidence or the implausibility of the events, but the philosophical presuppositions that exclude the possibility of the supernatural. This presupposition creates a chasm between the biblical worldview, which acknowledges a God who acts in history, and the naturalistic worldview, which denies such a possibility. In the end, the question of miracles transcends the mere analysis of facts; it requires a consideration of the philosophical and theological foundations that undergird one's understanding of reality. For the believer, miracles are not only possible; they are expected signs of the living God who is actively involved in His creation.

Evaluating Naturalism in the Light of Biblical Events

When we consider the biblical events through the lens of naturalism, we confront a worldview that insists on a cosmos governed by fixed laws, where supernatural interventions are categorically denied. Naturalism, by its nature, precludes the possibility of miracles, defining them as violations of the natural order. However, the Bible presents a different paradigm—one in which Jehovah, the Creator of the natural order, actively intervenes in His creation.

Miracles as Events Beyond Natural Law

The crux of naturalism's difficulty with biblical events is rooted in its presupposition that all events are explainable through natural causes. Miracles such as the parting of the Red Sea (*Yam Suf*, יַם־סוּף), the sun standing still in Joshua's time (Joshua 10:12-14), and Jesus walking on water

(Matthew 14:25) are not just improbable within this framework; they are dismissed outright. The naturalist sees these events as the product of pre-scientific, mythological thinking rather than historical realities.

Historicity and Miraculous Events

The historical claims of the Bible are numerous, and they include detailed accounts of miraculous events. The historicity of these events is affirmed not just by the biblical text but by the actions and beliefs of those who witnessed them. For instance, the early Christian community's rapid growth, its members' willingness to face persecution, and the transformation of skeptics such as Paul (*Sha'ul*, שָׁאוּל) are indirect attestations to the reality of the events they witnessed.

Intersecting Faith and Reason

A conservative approach to Scripture does not seek to undermine reason but rather to recognize the limitations of human understanding when it comes to the divine. While naturalism holds that reason is the ultimate arbiter of truth, a biblical worldview understands that reason itself was created by Jehovah and is therefore not the final authority on what is possible for Him. Faith and reason intersect in the biblical accounts, providing a coherent and intellectually viable perspective that acknowledges God's transcendent power.

The Philosophical Presuppositions of Naturalism

Naturalism carries philosophical presuppositions that impact its interpretation of all phenomena. By assuming that miracles cannot occur, it limits its understanding of the universe to what can be empirically verified. This approach, however, runs into problems when it encounters historical events that are substantiated by reliable witnesses but include elements that transcend natural explanations. The Bible asserts that Jehovah is not bound by the laws He created; hence, miracles are not violations of natural law but rather expressions of divine will.

Miracles as Signs and Wonders

In the Hebrew Scriptures, the term for wonders, *mopheth* (מוֹפֵת), is often used in conjunction with signs. These signs served to validate the message of Jehovah's prophets and, ultimately, the authority of Jesus as the Messiah (*Mashiach*, מָשִׁיחַ). The Gospel accounts utilize the term *ergon* (ἔργον), typically translated as "works," to describe Jesus's miraculous deeds. These works were not merely displays of power but were also emblematic of the in-breaking of God's kingdom, acting as foretastes of the restoration Jehovah promises.

The Purpose of Miracles in Scripture

In the biblical narrative, miracles serve specific purposes: they are acts of compassion, signs of the coming kingdom, and validations of Jehovah's messengers. For example, the miracle of feeding the 5,000 (Mark 6:34-44) not only addressed immediate physical needs but also pointed to Jesus as the true *bread of life* (John 6:35). In this and other miracles, Jesus's actions were not random displays of power but targeted interventions that revealed the nature and character of God.

Jehovah's Sovereignty Over Creation

The Bible presents Jehovah as sovereign over creation, not as a deistic watchmaker who winds up the universe and steps away. This sovereignty implies the ability to intervene at will. The miracles described in the Scriptures are not anomalies but demonstrations of this sovereignty. When Jesus calmed the storm (Mark 4:39), it was an affirmation that even the winds and the sea obey him.

Miracles and the Foundational Period of the Christian Congregation

The miraculous events recorded in the Bible are not uniformly distributed throughout history but are concentrated at pivotal moments, particularly during the foundational period of the Christian congregation. The apostolic miracles served to establish the fledgling church and authenticate the apostolic message. Once the Scriptures were penned and widely disseminated, the foundational role of miracles, as seen in the first century, ceased. The necessity for miracles diminished as the written Word of Jehovah became the primary means by which faith was to be engendered and nurtured.

In sum, evaluating naturalism in the light of biblical events requires a paradigm shift for the naturalist. It requires acknowledging that if there is a God like Jehovah, who is omnipotent and sovereign over His creation, then miracles are not only possible but also consistent with His revealed character and purposes. While the cessationist view acknowledges that the age of biblical miracles—those signs and wonders performed by Jesus and the apostles—has passed, it does not limit Jehovah's ability to act in history. It simply recognizes that His methods have changed in accordance with His divine will and the maturity of the Christian congregation. The historical-grammatical method of interpretation applied to the biblical text supports this view, affirming that while miracles have served their purpose, Jehovah's Word now stands as the ultimate testimony to His will and purposes for humanity.

CHAPTER 5 Nature and Supernature

Defining the Domains: Nature and Supernature in Biblical Context

In the sacred text of the Bible, the domains of nature and supernature are distinctly defined, yet they are intricately related in the unfolding of Jehovah's sovereign plan. Nature, or the created order, operates according to laws established by Jehovah at creation. Supernature, on the other hand, refers to that which is above or beyond nature; it is the realm of the divine, encompassing Jehovah's attributes and actions that transcend human understanding and the created order.

The Biblical View of Nature

The biblical narrative begins with the affirmation of nature's creation: "In the beginning, Jehovah created the heavens and the earth" (Genesis 1:1). Nature is depicted as a complex system designed with purpose and precision. The Hebrew word for "create," *bara* (בָּרָא), implies bringing something into existence that has never existed before. This creative act establishes the laws of nature, which are consistent and reliable, reflecting the orderliness of Jehovah's character.

Nature's Laws as Jehovah's Servants

Nature's laws are not independent forces; they are described as servants of Jehovah, performing His word: "He sends forth His command to the earth; His word runs very swiftly. He gives snow like wool; He scatters the frost like ashes" (Psalm 147:15-16). The regularity and predictability of natural laws are testimony to the wisdom and authority of Jehovah, not evidence of a universe absent His ongoing concern and control.

Supernature: The Realm of the Divine

Supernature, or the supernatural realm, is where Jehovah's unlimited power (*dunamis*, δύναμις) is fully manifest. The supernatural is not an aberration or a contradiction of the natural but is, instead, a higher dimension of reality. Miracles, as supernatural events, are explicit interventions by Jehovah into the natural world, revealing His dominion over both the natural and the supernatural realms.

The Significance of Miracles

Miracles, in the biblical context, are not merely wonders to amaze but signs to instruct and guide. They serve a revelatory purpose, pointing beyond themselves to divine truths. When Jesus performed miracles, such as healing the blind or raising the dead, these were not simply suspensions of natural laws but were expressions of Jehovah's purposes. For instance, when Jesus restored sight to the man born blind (John 9:1-7), it was not only a physical healing but also a spiritual sign illuminating Jesus as the light of the world (*phos tou kosmou*, φῶς τοῦ κόσμου).

Integration of Nature and Supernature in the Biblical Narrative

In the biblical account, nature and supernature are not isolated domains; they are integrated in the person and work of Jesus. The incarnation itself—the Word becoming flesh (John 1:14)—is the ultimate union of the natural and the supernatural. Jesus entered into the physical world, subjecting Himself to its conditions while also manifesting His divine nature through supernatural acts.

Miracles as Foretastes of the Future Kingdom

The miracles of Jesus are not just interventions in the natural order but are also foretastes of the future kingdom where Jehovah will fully establish His reign. The miracle of the resurrection is the pinnacle of this, as Jesus's victory over death (*thanatos*, θάνατος) is a preview of the future resurrection hope promised to believers (1 Corinthians 15:20-22).

The Cessation of Miraculous Gifts

In the context of biblical history, miracles had a foundational role, especially in establishing the early Christian congregation. The miraculous gifts of the Holy Spirit, as witnessed in the first-century church, were intended for that formative period. As the canon of Scripture was completed, the need for these miraculous gifts receded. This is not to suggest Jehovah's power has diminished or that He cannot perform miracles today, but rather that the primary means through which He speaks to

His people is through His Word, not through ongoing miraculous signs.

The Role of Faith in Understanding Nature and Supernature

Faith is the means by which believers apprehend truths about both nature and supernature. It is through faith that one understands that "the worlds were framed by the word of Jehovah, so that what is seen was not made out of things which are visible" (Hebrews 11:3). Faith does not reject the natural order but sees in it the handiwork of Jehovah and recognizes His prerogative to act within it supernaturally.

The Limits of Human Understanding

While Jehovah has revealed much about Himself and His works, there remains an element of mystery. Human understanding, even when informed by revelation, is limited. There are aspects of Jehovah's workings in the realms of nature and supernature that transcend human comprehension. The book of Job powerfully illustrates this point, as Jehovah speaks out of the whirlwind to remind Job of the vastness of His creation and the limits of human knowledge (Job 38–41).

In summary, the biblical framework presents nature as the realm created and sustained by Jehovah, operating according to His established laws, and supernature as the realm of Jehovah's unlimited power and divine mysteries. While miracles—as supernatural acts—are primarily historical, they continue to hold theological significance, testifying to Jehovah's sovereignty over all creation and His ultimate purposes for humanity. Faith is crucial in navigating the interplay between these two domains, grounding belief in the reality of Jehovah's actions in history and trust in His unfathomable wisdom.

Interplay of Divine Power and Natural Order

In the tapestry of biblical theology, the interplay between divine power and natural order is both profound and essential. This interplay is evident in the narratives of Scripture where the extraordinary actions of Jehovah—miracles—punctuate the canvas of human history, manifesting His sovereign will and purposes. These divine acts serve as markers, pointing to pivotal moments when Jehovah's intervention is clear and decisive.

The Foundation of Natural Law

The Scriptures affirm that the universe operates according to consistent principles or laws, which are decreed by Jehovah. The concept of natural law is foundational to understanding how the world functions. The Psalmist declares, "Jehovah has established His throne in the heavens, and His kingdom rules over all" (Psalm 103:19). Natural laws are not merely physical but are undergirded by Jehovah's sovereign rule. They provide the regularity and predictability necessary for life and are a reflection of Jehovah's faithfulness and His covenant with creation (Jeremiah 33:25).

Divine Power as a Means of Revelation

Divine power, or *dunamis* (δύναμις), transcends natural law and is frequently displayed in the Bible through miraculous events. Jehovah's power is not an arbitrary force but a means of revelation. It reveals His character, His purposes, and His care for creation. The miracles performed by Jehovah in the Old Testament, such as parting the Red Sea (Exodus 14:21-22) or stopping the sun in the sky during Joshua's battle (Joshua 10:12-13), are examples of divine power that reveal Jehovah's commitment to His people.

The Continuity and Discontinuity of Divine Acts

While the natural order continues with regularity, divine interventions represent moments of discontinuity, where the normal operation of the world is overruled or suspended. This discontinuity, however, does not imply chaos or the abrogation of natural law; rather, it signifies Jehovah's direct involvement in the course of human events. These miraculous events are special instances where Jehovah's purposes require a departure from the ordinary processes of nature to demonstrate His sovereignty and to accomplish His redemptive plans.

Miracles as Affirmations of Prophetic Authority

In the biblical account, miracles often serve as validations of prophetic authority. When Elijah calls down fire from heaven on Mount Carmel (1 Kings 18:37-38), it is not merely a display of power but a confirmation of his status as Jehovah's prophet and a challenge to the idolatry of the people. Similarly, the miracles performed by Jesus are not random acts of power but serve to validate His identity as the Messiah and the Son of God. They affirm the authenticity of His message and His authority to inaugurate the Kingdom of Jehovah.

The Miracles of Jesus and the Messianic Age

The miracles of Jesus are central to the Gospel narratives. They are signs that the Messianic age has dawned and that Jehovah's kingdom is breaking into the world in a new and powerful way. When Jesus heals the sick, raises the dead, or calms the stormy sea, these are not merely suspensions of natural laws but eschatological signs that the restoration of all things has begun (Acts 3:21). Jesus's miracles are thus both historical events and eschatological in their significance.

The Transition from Sign to Substance

With the close of the apostolic age and the completion of the New Testament canon, the function of miracles as signs transitions from the foreground to the background. The early miraculous gifts of the Spirit served their purpose in authenticating the apostolic message and the nascent church. As the written Word of Jehovah became established and disseminated, the need for these authenticating signs decreased. The focus shifts from the sign to the substance, from miracles to the message of salvation and sanctification through Jesus Christ.

The Role of Providence in the Natural Order

Even as the occurrence of overt miracles recedes, the doctrine of providence affirms Jehovah's continuous, sovereign, and purposeful upholding of all things. Providence is Jehovah's governance of the world, in which He sustains the natural order, cooperates with everything that happens, and guides the universe to its appointed end. This governance is not less divine because it operates through natural laws; indeed, the regularity of those laws is a testament to Jehovah's faithful providence.

Miracles and Faith in the Sovereignty of Jehovah

The Bible does not encourage a pursuit of miracles but rather a faith in the sovereignty and providence of Jehovah. The believer's trust is not in the extraordinary and the spectacular but in the sure promises of Jehovah and the redemptive work of Jesus Christ. Faith recognizes that Jehovah is as present in the natural order as He is in the supernatural intervention. It understands that the same power that parted the Red Sea is at work in the unfolding of history and the transformation of lives.

Concluding Thoughts on Nature and Supernature

In conclusion, the biblical narrative portrays a world that is intrinsically good and orderly, governed by laws established by Jehovah. Within this world, miracles serve a specific purpose in the unfolding of Jehovah's redemptive plan. While the age of miracles as signs has passed, the power of Jehovah remains active in the world through His providence. The divine power that once interrupted the natural order now sustains it, guiding creation towards its ultimate purpose—a new creation where Jehovah will dwell with His people forever. Thus, the believer lives in anticipation, not of miracles, but of the fulfillment of Jehovah's promise of a new heaven and a new earth, where righteousness dwells (2 Peter 3:13).

Biblical Miracles: When Nature Bends to Supernature

In the canon of Scripture, the occurrence of miracles serves as a testament to moments when the natural realm yields to the supremacy of the supernatural—when the ordinary laws that govern our world are transcended by divine intervention. This intersection between nature and supernature is not a mere backdrop for storytelling but is rather a substantive element within the biblical revelation, highlighting the sovereign dominion of Jehovah and His active participation in the history of redemption.

The Significance of the Supernatural in Scripture

Within the sacred texts, the supernatural is not an occasional oddity but a deliberate manifestation of divine power—*dunamis* (δύναμις)—intervening in human affairs. These interventions are indicators of something beyond themselves; they are signs pointing to Jehovah's covenantal faithfulness, judgment, and mercy. The Israelites' exodus from Egypt, replete with plagues such as the transformation of water into blood (Exodus 7:17-20), the plague of darkness (Exodus 10:21-23), and the parting of the Red Sea (Exodus 14:21-22), are archetypal instances where natural laws are superseded by the direct act of Jehovah to redeem His people and to judge the oppressive powers of the world.

Creation Responding to Its Creator

In the biblical accounts, nature itself is often depicted as being responsive to the voice of its Creator. For instance, the account of Joshua's long day, where the sun stood still

(Joshua 10:12-13), presents a picture of the cosmos obedient to the command of Jehovah, reinforcing the truth that all creation is subject to His will. Such narratives do not reflect a mythology or a pre-scientific worldview but rather articulate a theological truth: Jehovah is Lord over creation, and at His command, the natural order can be altered.

Miracles as Demonstrations of Divine Authority

Miracles within the Bible also serve as expressions of divine authority and messianic authentication. Jesus's miracles, such as turning water into wine at Cana (John 2:7-11), feeding the five thousand (Matthew 14:19-21), and the resurrection of Lazarus (John 11:43-44), are emblematic of His divine authority and messianic identity. These miracles are supernatural acts that confirm His teachings and provide a foretaste of the coming eschatological kingdom, where there will be a restoration of all things.

Healing and the Restoration of Creation

The healing miracles performed by Jesus are not only compassionate responses to human suffering but also signs of the kingdom of Jehovah breaking into the present age. When Jesus heals the blind, the lame, and the leprous, these acts of restoration signify the beginning of the new creation, where the effects of the fall are reversed. The language used in these narratives often conveys a restoration to an intended order, as in the healing of the man with the withered hand (Mark 3:1-5), where the word *apokatastasis* (ἀποκατάστασις), meaning restoration to an original condition, underscores the supernatural restoration power of Jehovah through Jesus.

Miracles and the Prophetic Message

The prophets of old performed miracles not merely as proofs of personal power but as validations of their message from Jehovah. Elijah's and Elisha's miracles, including the raising of the widow's son (1 Kings 17:22) and the purification of the poisoned stew (2 Kings 4:41), respectively, were signs that authenticated their prophetic office and underscored the words they spoke as being truly from Jehovah.

The Eschatological Dimension of Miracles

Miracles have an eschatological dimension, pointing forward to the ultimate restoration of all things. The Book of Revelation, with its vivid imagery of a new heaven and a new earth (Revelation 21:1), culminates the biblical narrative by looking forward to the time when the supernatural will fully and finally heal the natural order. The miracles recorded in Scripture are glimpses and guarantees of this promised renewal, where death and mourning will be no more, and Jehovah will dwell with His people.

The Transition from Miracles to the Word

As the early Christian congregation established itself and the canon of Scripture was completed, the role of miracles as foundational and confirmatory signs began to transition. The completed written Word—the Bible—became the primary means through which Jehovah's will was made known. The epistles and the Gospel accounts provided the necessary instruction, correction, and encouragement for the congregation, and thus, the reliance on miracles as evidence of divine intervention decreased.

The apostolic teachings, now inscribed in Scripture, became the guide and authority for faith and practice.

Miracles and Modern Faith

The cessation of the miraculous gifts and events, as commonly recorded in the New Testament, coincides with the cessation of the revelatory process. This does not suggest that Jehovah is no longer at work in the world but rather that His works are now primarily through providence rather than miraculous intervention. It also underscores the sufficiency of Scripture, which thoroughly equips the believer for every good work (2 Timothy 3:16-17). The miracles of Scripture continue to serve as foundational testimonies of Jehovah's intervention in history, providing the framework within which believers understand their faith and the world around them.

In the narrative of Scripture, miracles are the points where the natural order pauses, allowing supernature to be vividly seen. They are the moments when the curtain between heaven and earth is drawn back, and Jehovah's presence and power are undeniably displayed. They provide not only a historical record of divine intervention but also theological insight into the character of Jehovah and His redemptive purposes. While miracles in the biblical sense are not a present expectation, the same divine power that acted in history is believed to be at work today, directing the unfolding of Jehovah's providential plan.

The Coexistence of Natural Laws and Supernatural Acts

In the scriptural narrative, natural laws and supernatural acts coexist in a manner that is often mysterious to the human mind. This coexistence underlines a world that operates consistently under Jehovah's established ordinances while also being subject to His immediate and extraordinary intervention. The exploration of this coexistence involves delving into the understanding of how Jehovah, who set the natural laws in place, also intervenes in them for specific divine purposes.

Natural Laws as Jehovah's Ordinances

Natural laws, the regular patterns and principles observed in creation, are described in Scripture as being established by Jehovah Himself. The book of Jeremiah refers to the fixed order of heaven and earth which Jehovah has set (Jeremiah 31:35). This fixed order is not a distant, deistic reality but a dynamic framework through which Jehovah governs the universe. It is expressed in the Hebrew word *ḥoq* (חֹק), which indicates something inscribed or decreed, a term that conveys the stability and reliability of the natural order as it upholds creation.

Supernatural Acts Breaking into the Natural Realm

On the other hand, supernatural acts—those events which interrupt the usual course of nature—demonstrate that Jehovah is not bound by the laws He Himself has decreed. For example, the account of Elijah's prayer for rain, which ended a long drought (1 Kings 18:41-45), shows how the natural process of weather patterns can be overridden by divine command. This intervention demonstrates *dunamis* (δύναμις), the power of Jehovah to alter natural processes according to His sovereign will.

Miracles: Signposts of Redemption

The miracles performed by Jesus, especially those involving control over nature, such as calming a storm (Mark 4:39), underscore the belief that while nature operates under Jehovah's laws, it is also the arena for His redemptive actions. These miracles serve as signposts pointing to the reality of the kingdom of Jehovah breaking into the world, affirming that the natural realm is subject to the authority of Christ, who upholds all things by His powerful word (Hebrews 1:3).

The Harmony of Natural and Supernatural

It is vital to understand that in the biblical perspective, natural laws and supernatural acts are not in conflict; instead, they represent different aspects of Jehovah's rule over creation. The Psalmist declares that the heavens are telling of the glory of Jehovah; the skies display His handiwork (Psalm 19:1). The regularity of nature reveals Jehovah's glory, while the supernatural interruptions manifest His immediate presence and power.

Purpose Behind Supernatural Interventions

When miracles occur in the Bible, they are not random displays of power but purposeful acts intended to reveal divine truths, establish Jehovah's covenant, and propel His redemptive plan forward. For instance, the miracle of the virgin birth of Jesus (Matthew 1:23) points to the incarnation, where the natural process of human birth is overshadowed by the supernatural act of the Holy Spirit, ensuring that the Messiah is both fully divine and fully human, fulfilling the prophecy from Isaiah.

The Foundational Role of Miracles in Scripture

In the biblical account, miracles played a foundational role during formative periods—such as the Exodus, the ministries of Elijah and Elisha, and the life of Jesus— serving as signs and wonders to validate the message and messengers of Jehovah. In the early Christian congregation, miracles by the apostles served a similar foundational role, affirming the truth of the Gospel and the presence of Jehovah's power among His people (Hebrews 2:3-4).

Transition from Miracles to Providence

As the scriptural canon closed with the Revelation given to John, the narrative of miracles serving as the primary means of divine revelation gave way to a reliance on Jehovah's providential guidance. Providence refers to Jehovah's governance of all events in the universe that maintains the existence and activity within creation. While it operates within the natural order, it is no less a demonstration of Jehovah's ongoing care and involvement in His creation.

Theological Implications for Believers

For believers, this understanding requires a trust in the sufficiency of Scripture and in Jehovah's sovereign control over both natural laws and supernatural acts. The cessation of widespread miraculous events as recorded in Scripture points to a matured understanding of faith, where the believer's confidence rests not on the visible and extraordinary, but on the assurances of Jehovah's Word and His unfailing providence.

Miracles as Historical Testimonies

While contemporary Christians may not witness the miracles as the early church did, these historical testimonies continue to fortify faith. They serve as enduring witnesses to Jehovah's past interventions and give hope for the future consummation of His kingdom, as promised in Scripture. This perspective anchors the believer's hope not in the longing for miraculous signs but in the trustworthiness of Jehovah who is the same yesterday, today, and forever (Hebrews 13:8).

In sum, the biblical portrayal of miracles does not diminish the reality of the natural laws established by Jehovah but rather enhances it by demonstrating that above and beyond these laws is a God who is personally involved in His creation. This personal involvement was supremely manifested in the person and work of Jesus Christ, and it continues to be manifest in the life of the church through the guiding principles of Scripture and the providential workings of Jehovah. The coexistence of natural laws and supernatural acts within the Bible serves as a testament to Jehovah's sovereign power and His ultimate authority over all creation.

CHAPTER 6 The Difficulty in Naturalism

Exploring the Inconsistencies: Naturalism's Struggle with Miracles

Naturalism, the belief that everything arises from natural properties and causes, and supernatural or spiritual explanations are not necessary, has had a longstanding tension with the concept of miracles. This worldview asserts that the laws of nature are fixed and that all phenomena can be explained through these laws and empirical observation. The miraculous, by its very nature, contradicts the core premises of naturalism, presenting a notable point of contention between the naturalistic perspective and the biblical narrative.

The Foundation of Naturalism

Naturalism rests on the presupposition that nature is a closed, self-sustaining system. This means that natural causes are the only kind of causes that exist, and hence, natural causes can only produce natural effects. In this view, miracles are often dismissed a priori because they presuppose an intervention that violates the perceived consistent and unalterable laws of nature. Yet, the challenge arises when the comprehensive explanatory power of naturalism is confronted with historical accounts of miracles.

Historical Accounts and Miraculous Claims

The Scriptures present miracles not as literary devices or allegories but as historical events with real-time witnesses. For instance, the resurrection of Jesus Christ is a pivotal event recounted with multiple eyewitness accounts. This event, foundational to Christian faith, stands in direct opposition to the naturalistic assertion that dead men do not rise. The Greek term *anastasis* (ἀνάστασις) describes this resurrection, emphasizing a literal, bodily rising.

Naturalism's Interpretative Limitations

The limitation of naturalism becomes evident when it encounters the narrative of miracles such as the virgin birth, the turning of water into wine, or the parting of the Red Sea. These events are problematic for naturalism because they do not fit within the framework of empirical investigation and repeatability. They are unique, non-repeatable acts of Jehovah, which from a naturalistic viewpoint, are either impossible or must be explained away or reinterpreted.

Philosophical Considerations

From a philosophical standpoint, naturalism is also challenged by the concept of induction—the belief that the future will resemble the past. This principle is foundational to the naturalistic reliance on the uniformity of nature. However, if we consider that miracles could have occurred, the principle of induction is not sufficient to categorically preclude such events. David Hume, an 18th-century philosopher and skeptic, argued against the possibility of miracles, yet his arguments rested on the presupposition of unvarying natural laws, which is itself a point of philosophical debate.

Miracles as a Logical Possibility

Even within a naturalistic framework, there is a logical possibility for the occurrence of miracles if one admits that our understanding of the natural world is not exhaustive. Given that new laws of nature have been discovered throughout history and our understanding of the universe continues to evolve, it is theoretically possible that events currently considered miraculous could be understood differently in the future. However, this concession does not sit comfortably within strict naturalism, which tends to resist any explanation outside of natural laws.

Miracles and the Historical-Grammatical Method

In contrast to naturalism, the historical-grammatical method of biblical interpretation acknowledges the presence of the supernatural as a real and essential aspect of the biblical narrative. This method takes into account the historical context, literary genres, and the original languages of Scripture, providing a comprehensive framework for understanding biblical texts. For example, the Exodus narrative with its plagues, including *bara* (בָּרָד), the hail mixed with fire, is treated not just as an ancient myth but as a record of Jehovah's intervention in history.

Testimony of the Early Church

The early Christian church's rapid growth is often attributed to the testimony of miracles, signs, and wonders that accompanied the apostles' preaching. The healing of the lame man at the Beautiful Gate by Peter and John, described with the Greek term *iaomai* (ἰάομαι), meaning to heal, serves as an example. Such accounts hold significant historical weight, suggesting that naturalism's blanket denial of the miraculous is at odds with the lived experiences of early Christians.

Modern Implications

For the modern Christian, the implications of naturalism's struggle with miracles are profound. While miracles are not the everyday expectation for the believer, their historical occurrence underpins the Christian faith. The reliance on Scripture, the record of these miraculous events, provides the believer with a sense of continuity with the faith of the early church, a continuity that is not predicated on the continual repetition of the miraculous but on the enduring truth of Jehovah's word and deeds.

In conclusion, naturalism's attempt to reconcile with the biblical account of miracles reveals several inconsistencies. While naturalistic explanations strive to maintain a worldview confined to empirical and repeatable phenomena, the biblical narrative stands as a testament to a reality that encompasses more than the material world. It presents a universe where Jehovah's supernatural acts intersect with human history, affirming the Christian belief in a God who is both transcendent and immanent. Thus, while naturalism may grapple with the concept of miracles, the biblical perspective accepts them as part of the fabric of divine revelation, central to the understanding of Jehovah's interaction with creation and His ultimate purpose for humanity.

Naturalism's Limits in Accounting for Biblical Wonders

The biblical narrative is replete with accounts of wonders and miracles that defy naturalistic explanations. Naturalism, with its insistence on material causes and effects, reaches its limits when confronted with these biblical wonders. These events are not merely extraordinary; they are expressions of the divine will that interrupt the regular pattern of nature.

The Nature of Biblical Miracles

Biblical miracles are acts of Jehovah that signify his sovereign power over creation. They are not hidden or subtle, but are instead overt displays intended to affirm divine authority and purpose. They frequently serve as turning points in the biblical narrative, moments where the natural course of events is suspended, and Jehovah's intervention is unmistakable.

Miracles in the Hebrew Scriptures

In the Hebrew Scriptures, miracles often occur in contexts where Jehovah is confirming His covenant, delivering His people, or demonstrating His superiority over false gods. For example, during the Exodus, the ten plagues, including the turning of the Nile to blood (*dam* - דָּם), not only pressure Pharaoh to release the Israelites but also challenge the Egyptian gods, who were believed to control the Nile and other aspects of nature.

The Miracles of Jesus

In the New Testament, Jesus performs miracles that not only alleviate suffering but also authenticate his claims about his identity and mission. When he calms the stormy sea, he uses the Greek word *siōpaō* (σιωπάω) meaning "to be silent" or "be still", demonstrating his authority over the natural world. This and other miracles like healing the blind and raising the dead stand in contrast to the naturalistic perspective, which would assert such events cannot occur because they violate the known laws of physics and biology.

Naturalistic Explanations Fall Short

When naturalists approach the miracles of the Bible, they often try to find explanations that fit within a closed system of cause and effect. For instance, some have tried to explain the parting of the Red Sea as a natural phenomenon caused by wind patterns. However, these explanations fail to account for the timing and specific details described in the biblical text, such as the Israelites crossing on dry ground and the waters returning at the precise moment to thwart the Egyptian army.

The Philosophical Implications of Denying Miracles

To maintain a naturalistic worldview in the face of biblical miracles, one must adopt a philosophy that either outright denies the supernatural or reinterprets the biblical text to fit a naturalistic mold. This approach not only alters the intended meaning of the Scriptures but also implies that the experiences and testimonies of those who witnessed these events were either mistaken or deceptive.

Historical Authenticity and Eyewitness Testimony

The biblical accounts of miracles come with claims of historical authenticity and eyewitness testimony. For instance, the resurrection of Jesus is not presented as a mythological tale but as an event witnessed by many individuals whose lives were transformed as a result. The apostle Paul, in his first letter to the Corinthians, refers to over five hundred witnesses who saw the risen Christ, offering a bold invitation to verify the claim with those who were still alive.

The Resurrection: A Stumbling Block for Naturalism

The resurrection stands as the most formidable challenge to naturalism. The Greek term *anastasis* (ἀνάστασις) is used consistently to refer to a physical, bodily resurrection. Naturalism has no framework to account for this event because it fundamentally alters the nature of reality. If Jesus truly rose from the dead, then naturalism is inadequate to explain the world and our existence in it.

Miracles as Foretastes of the Future Kingdom

Biblical miracles are often viewed as foretastes of the future kingdom, where the effects of sin and the curse are reversed. For instance, Isaiah speaks of a time when the eyes of the blind will be opened and the ears of the deaf unstopped (*pathach* - פָּתַח for "open" in Isaiah 35:5). These miracles offer a glimpse of what Jehovah intends for creation, where the natural order is restored to its original perfection.

The Role of Faith in Understanding Miracles

From a biblical perspective, understanding miracles is not merely an intellectual exercise; it involves faith. Faith is the means by which believers accept the reality of miracles, not as violations of nature, but as acts of Jehovah who is the author of nature. Faith accepts that Jehovah, who established the laws of nature, is not bound by them.

The biblical wonders represent a significant challenge to the naturalistic worldview. While naturalism demands a closed system of cause and effect, the Bible presents a dynamic interaction between Jehovah and His creation, which includes the suspension of natural laws for divine purposes. Biblical miracles invite us to expand our understanding of reality to include the divine, where Jehovah's will operates not only through natural processes but also, at times, independently of them. These wonders serve as testimony to His power and sovereignty, and while they may be historical, their impact and the truth they attest to are timeless.

The Problem of Dismissing the Supernatural

In a world where the empirical and measurable are often valued above all else, the supernatural elements of the Bible can be met with skepticism. The dismissal of the supernatural is not merely a rejection of biblical accounts as myth; it is an ideological stance that can reshape one's entire approach to the Bible and its teachings.

The Undermining of Biblical Authority

Dismissing the supernatural begins with a presupposition that events which defy natural laws simply cannot occur, which directly challenges the veracity of biblical narrative. Take, for instance, the resurrection of Lazarus (John 11:43-44). If one rejects the possibility that Jesus could raise a man from the dead, this rejection doesn't only dismiss the event itself, but it also calls into question the authority of the Gospel of John and, by extension, the entire biblical canon.

The Significance of Miracles to the Gospel Message

The miracles of Jesus, such as the feeding of the five thousand (*trophe* - τροφή for "food" in John 6:11) and turning water into wine at Cana (*huparchō* - ὑπάρχω for "turning" in John 2:9), are not peripheral to the Gospel message—they are central. These acts display his divine nature and authority, and to dismiss them is to disregard a key element of Jesus's identity and mission. The Gospel writers, aware of the unique nature of Jesus's works, used terms like *semeion* (σημεῖον) to describe his miracles, emphasizing that they were signs pointing to a greater reality.

The Diminished Role of Prophecy

Prophecy is another aspect of the supernatural within the Bible that naturalism struggles to accommodate. Prophetic foresight, such as Isaiah's detailed description of the suffering servant (Isaiah 53), which Christians understand as pointing to Christ, becomes inexplicable if the supernatural is dismissed. Without the recognition of supernatural revelation, the accuracy of such prophecies is often relegated to after-the-fact writing or coincidence.

The Historical Reality of Miracles

The Bible records miracles as historical events. The parting of the Jordan River for Joshua and the Israelites (*nāhar* - נָהָר for "river" in Joshua 3:16) and the collapse of the walls of Jericho (*chomah* - חוֹמָה for "wall" in Joshua 6:20) are not presented as allegories or myths but as real occurrences witnessed by the people of Israel. The biblical writers imbue these accounts with the weight of historical events, grounding the miraculous in the temporal and tangible world.

The Ontological Nature of Miracles

Miracles, in the biblical sense, are ontological phenomena—they relate to the very nature of being and reality. When Jesus heals the blind man (*typhlos* - τυφλὸς for "blind" in John 9:1), it is not merely a physical restoration, but an ontological transformation from darkness to light, both physically and spiritually. By denying the supernatural, one also denies a key way in which the Bible communicates God's interaction with and transformation of reality.

The Personal Testimony of Believers

The personal testimony of individuals who claim to have experienced the supernatural presents a challenge to the naturalistic framework. For instance, the transformation of Saul to Paul (Acts 9:1-19), which involved a direct encounter with the risen Christ, is a powerful personal testimony that transcends mere subjective experience; it had tangible effects on Paul's life and mission. The naturalistic view must either discredit these personal experiences or interpret them as psychological phenomena, thus reducing profound life changes to mere epiphenomena of brain activity.

The Philosophical Inconsistency in Excluding the Supernatural

There is a philosophical inconsistency in the strict naturalistic approach. If one accepts the existence of abstract entities such as numbers, propositions, or even moral truths, which are not detectable by the scientific method, then on what grounds does one dismiss the supernatural? The inconsistency lies in the selective skepticism that accepts certain non-empirical realities but rejects others, like the biblical miracles, without sufficient justification.

Dismissing the supernatural from the Bible is not a neutral stance; it has profound implications for how one reads and understands Scripture. The biblical narrative is not only a record of natural events but also of the ways in which Jehovah has acted within and upon creation in ways that transcend our understanding of natural law. To remove the supernatural is to ignore the dimension of the divine that the Bible insists is real and active. It challenges the authenticity of the biblical accounts and weakens the message of the Bible, which portrays a world where the material and the spiritual are inextricably linked, with the supernatural acting as a testament to Jehovah's presence and power in the world.

Reconciling Miracles with a Naturalistic Worldview

In the pursuit to reconcile miracles with a naturalistic worldview, one must wrestle with the conviction that the natural world operates entirely on a set of unbreakable laws. This presents a considerable challenge to the acceptance of miracles, which by definition are occurrences that fall outside the realm of natural explanations.

Edward D. Andrews

The Predicament of Limiting Reality to Naturalism

The naturalistic worldview posits that all phenomena can be explained by natural causes and laws. However, this perspective faces a conundrum when confronted with biblical miracles. For example, consider the virgin birth of Jesus (Matthew 1:23), a foundational Christian belief that defies biological norms. The Greek term *parthenos* (παρθένος) signifies virgin, indicating a woman who has not known a man. Under a naturalistic lens, such an event is not possible, yet it is proclaimed as a pivotal truth within the biblical narrative.

The Intellectual Dissonance in Denying Biblical Miracles

Intellectual dissonance arises when one attempts to maintain a naturalistic framework while engaging with the biblical text. The miracles of Jesus, such as restoring sight to the blind or raising the dead, demand a departure from naturalistic constraints. The Greek term *dunamis* (δύναμις), often translated as "power" or "miracle," conveys an act that surpasses human capability and understanding. Dismissing these as mere myth or allegory fails to respect the intent of the biblical authors and the self-witness of the text.

The Historical-Critical Method and Miracles

The historical-critical method seeks to understand the Bible within its historical context. Yet, when it comes to miracles, this method often assumes a priori that supernatural events are impossible, thereby interpreting miraculous accounts as misunderstandings or fabrications of the ancient world. This approach overlooks the possibility that there may be more to reality than what is observable and measurable.

The Quest for Natural Explanations

Some scholars have attempted to reconcile miracles with naturalism by proposing natural explanations for biblical miracles. For instance, they may suggest a naturalistic cause for the parting of the Red Sea (*Yam Suf* - יַם סוּף in Exodus 14:21), such as a strong east wind. While such explanations may be appealing to a naturalistic worldview, they often do not fully account for the biblical description or the perceived meaning behind the event.

Miracles as the Inbreaking of the Divine

From a biblical perspective, miracles are understood as the inbreaking of the divine into the natural order. They are moments where Jehovah, according to His purposes, temporarily suspends or alters the normal functioning of the creation. For instance, the resurrection of Jesus (*anastasis* - ἀνάστασις in Mark 16:6), stands as the ultimate miracle, an event that transcends the naturalistic framework and serves as the cornerstone of Christian faith.

The Role of Faith in Understanding Miracles

Faith plays a central role in accepting biblical miracles. The Bible itself attests that faith is the assurance of things hoped for, the conviction of things not seen (Hebrews 11:1). This suggests that understanding and accepting miracles may not be possible through naturalistic reasoning alone, but through a posture of faith that opens one to the possibility of the supernatural.

The Epistemological Limitations of Naturalism

Naturalism, by its very nature, is epistemologically limited. It can only make claims about what is within the scope of natural observation and experimentation. Miracles, which are by nature supernatural, fall outside this scope, challenging the epistemological boundaries of a purely naturalistic worldview.

The Philosophical Acceptance of Supernatural Realities

Philosophically, one can argue for the acceptance of supernatural realities without abandoning reason or scientific inquiry. It requires an acknowledgment that science, while powerful in its domain, does not have a monopoly on truth. The acceptance of miracles does not necessitate the abandonment of naturalistic explanations where they apply, but rather an openness to the existence of realities beyond them.

The reconciliation of miracles with a naturalistic worldview is fraught with challenges, as it requires a fundamental openness to the possibility of the supernatural. The Bible presents miracles not as violations of the natural order but as testimonies to the power and purposes of Jehovah. While naturalism has greatly contributed to our understanding of the world, it may not be sufficient to fully grasp the multifaceted reality that includes the biblical accounts of miracles. Accepting miracles as part of the biblical narrative requires an epistemological humility that recognizes the limits of human understanding and the possibility that reality is broader and more mysterious than the naturalistic framework can encompass.

Edward D. Andrews

CHAPTER 7 Miracles and the Laws of Nature

Miracles in Biblical Perspective: Beyond Natural Law

In the biblical narrative, miracles are not mere embellishments but integral signs of Jehovah's sovereignty and purpose. They are instances where the observable, repeatable patterns of natural law are superseded— instances that the biblical writers describe with awe and reverence, fully aware of their extraordinary nature.

Defining 'Miracle' in a Biblical Context

The term "miracle" often evokes a variety of definitions, but within the framework of Scripture, it typically refers to an event or action that cannot be fully explained by natural causes. These are actions that point to the direct intervention of Jehovah, who is not bound by the physical laws He has created. The Hebrew term for miracle, *oth* (אוֹת), and the Greek *semeion* (σημεῖον), often translated as "sign," both suggest an occurrence that signifies something beyond itself, usually the hand of Jehovah or the validation of His messenger.

The Scope of Natural Law in Biblical Accounts

Natural law, as we understand it, comprises the observable phenomena and consistent patterns in the natural world. However, in the context of the Bible, these laws are not ultimate; they are subject to the authority of Jehovah. When Jesus turned water into wine at Cana (*John 2:1-11*), it was not a parlor trick or a manipulation of fermentation processes. It was a demonstration (*dunamis* - δύναμις) of His mastery over the natural order, revealing that the forces governing creation are subordinate to His will.

Miracles as Historical Realities within Scripture

Biblical authors present miracles as historical realities. When Jesus fed the 5,000 (*Matthew 14:13-21*), the Gospels do not treat this as a parable or metaphor, but as an actual event in time and space. The multiplication of loaves and fishes breaks the natural law of conservation of mass, emphasizing that, within the biblical perspective, Jehovah is not confined by the physical realities He has instituted.

The Interaction between Divine Will and Natural Law

The biblical worldview does not see a dichotomy between divine will and natural law; rather, it sees natural law as an expression of divine will. Thus, when natural law is transcended by a miracle, it is not a violation or a disruption, but rather a manifestation of divine will that transcends human understanding. For instance, the resurrection of Lazarus (*John 11:1-44*) was an event that reversed the irreversible law of biological death, displaying Jesus's authority over life and death.

Miracles as Foretastes of Future Reality

Miracles in the Bible also serve as foretastes of a future reality where Jehovah's purposes are fully realized. The healing miracles of Jesus not only alleviated immediate suffering but also pointed to the coming age where sickness and death will be no more (*Revelation 21:4*). The nature of these miracles suggests that they are signs pointing to the ultimate restoration of creation.

The Testament of Miracles to Jehovah's Character

Beyond their role as historical events, miracles also testify to the character of Jehovah. When He intervenes miraculously, it is not merely to showcase power but often to reveal aspects of His character—His mercy, His compassion, and His responsiveness to faith. The healing of the leper (*Mark 1:40-45*) is as much about the cleansing of disease as it is about the willingness of Jehovah to touch and restore the outcast.

The Fading of Miracles in Biblical Narrative

As mentioned in the mindset guiding this book, the occurrence of miracles in the biblical narrative diminishes as the written Word becomes more established. This suggests that miracles served specific purposes at specific times— often as signs to authenticate a message or messenger, such as the apostles in the early church (*2 Corinthians 12:12*). The progressive revelation of Jehovah's will through Scripture has lessened the need for such signs.

Miracles and the Faith of the Believer

For the believer, miracles are not necessarily expected to be a daily experience but are looked upon as reminders of Jehovah's past interventions and promises for the future. Faith does not hinge on the witnessing of miracles but rests on the trust in Jehovah's Word and character. Paul's discourse in *1 Corinthians 13* emphasizes that while prophecies and knowledge will pass away, faith, hope, and love remain.

In summary, miracles in the biblical context are not simply exceptions to natural law; they are profound affirmations of Jehovah's sovereignty over creation. They serve as signs of His presence and authority, testimonies of His will, and foretastes of a reality where His purposes are fully realized. While the naturalistic worldview seeks to explain reality solely by natural processes, the biblical perspective acknowledges a realm where Jehovah's will intersects with and transcends these processes.

The Sovereignty of Divine Acts Over Natural Laws

Within the biblical framework, the sovereignty of Jehovah over the natural world is incontrovertible. This sovereignty is profoundly manifested in the divine acts known as miracles, which, as recorded in the Scriptures, often intervene, overrule, and operate independently of the established natural laws. These acts serve as direct evidence of Jehovah's ultimate authority and power.

Divine Sovereignty Asserted in Creation

To understand the nature of miracles, it is essential to recognize that, according to the Bible, all natural laws are themselves expressions of Jehovah's will, established at creation. The very fabric of reality is spoken into being by His word (*dabar* - דָּבָר in Hebrew; *logos* - λόγος in Greek). *Genesis 1* describes this creative process, where Jehovah's commands give rise to the ordered universe, suggesting that the same voice that commanded "Let there be light" (*yehi 'or* - יְהִי אוֹר) is not confined by the physical laws that govern that created light.

Historical Testaments of Divine Supremacy

The Old Testament recounts multiple instances where Jehovah's actions directly contravene natural laws. One prime example is the parting of the Red Sea (*Exodus 14:21-22*), where the usual properties of water are temporarily suspended to allow the Israelites to escape Pharaoh's army. The waters stand as a wall (*chomah* - חוֹמָה), defying gravity and hydrodynamic principles, solely through Jehovah's command.

In the New Testament, Jesus's walking on water (*Matthew 14:25-26*) similarly defies the natural law of buoyancy and density. The miracle is not merely a display of power but a testament to the sovereignty of Jesus, who, as part of the divine nature, exercises authority over the laws of physics.

Miracles as Inbreakings of Divine Order

Miracles can be seen as inbreakings of a divine order into the natural one. They are not random acts of power but purposeful demonstrations of Jehovah's kingdom and order. The miraculous healings performed by Jesus, such as the restoration of the blind man's sight (*John 9:1-7*), do not just suspend biological processes but actually recreate or restore them to their intended state. Such acts reaffirm the biblical assertion that all things were created through and for the divine Logos (*Colossians 1:16*).

Miracles Contrasted with Magic or Myth

In the biblical account, miracles are distinct from the magical or mythological manipulations of nature common in other ancient narratives. While magic attempts to control or harness supernatural forces, biblical miracles are acts initiated by Jehovah's sovereign will. They are not techniques or spells subject to human will but are divine initiatives that human beings witness and to which they respond.

Prophetic Significance of Miracles

Many miracles in the Bible also carry prophetic significance. The healing miracles of Jesus are not just physical restorations but signal the inauguration of the Messianic age, where Jehovah's rule brings wholeness and life. These acts illustrate that Jesus is the promised Messiah (*haMashiach* - הַמָּשִׁיחַ), with authority to initiate the eschatological age foretold by the prophets.

The Role of Faith in the Narrative of Miracles

In the biblical accounts, miracles often intersect with the element of faith. While Jehovah's ability to perform miracles is not contingent on human belief, the New

Testament frequently highlights faith as a critical component in the occurrence of miracles. For instance, the woman with the issue of blood is healed because of her faith (*pistis* - πίστις) in Jesus's ability to heal her (*Mark 5:34*).

The End of the Age of Miracles

As this book's perspective emphasizes, the age of public miracles described in the Bible comes to an end with the establishment of the early church and the completion of the canon of Scripture. Miracles had a foundational role in confirming the authority of Jesus and His apostles (*2 Corinthians 12:12*). As the Scriptures became available, providing a complete and authoritative revelation of Jehovah's will, the function that miracles served in authenticating new revelation was no longer necessary.

Miracles in Modern Belief and Practice

While the era of biblical miracles as public spectacles has ceased, the possibility of Jehovah acting in ways that surpass human understanding is not denied. The focus for contemporary believers is on the sufficiency of Scripture and the ongoing work of Jehovah in the lives of individuals and communities, often in ways that are not outwardly miraculous but are nonetheless a part of His sovereign will.

In summation, miracles, as depicted in the Bible, are dramatic affirmations of Jehovah's sovereignty over all creation, including the natural laws. They serve specific divine purposes in the historical unfolding of Jehovah's plan, illustrating that while He often works within the created order, He is not subject to it. The cessation of the age of miracles does not imply the cessation of divine action but rather a shift in how Jehovah interacts with His creation, with the focus now on His Word and providence.

Understanding Biblical Miracles in a Scientific Age

In our contemporary era, marked by scientific discovery and empirical understanding, the concept of miracles as presented in the Bible may seem antithetical to the laws of nature as we understand them. This apparent dichotomy between faith and reason poses a significant challenge for believers and skeptics alike. To reconcile these views, it is crucial to delve deeply into the biblical text and the essence of what constitutes a miracle in the biblical context, all the while recognizing the lens through which we view the world has shifted dramatically since the time these texts were penned.

Miracles Through the Prism of Modern Science

The scientific method is built upon observable, repeatable, and predictable phenomena. When biblical miracles are examined under this lens, they defy natural explanations and sit outside the boundaries of scientific verification. This does not invalidate the biblical account; rather, it underscores the distinctiveness of miracles as acts of Jehovah that transcend the natural order. In biblical terms, a miracle (*semeion* in Greek - σημεῖον) is a sign that points beyond itself to divine truth or action.

Reconciling Biblical Accounts with Scientific Understanding

In the case of Jesus turning water into wine (*John 2:1-11*), the process violates the natural fermentation process as understood by chemistry. In this context, the biblical scholar would emphasize that the miracle is not an act that can be parsed out by chemical equations but a demonstration of divine authority over the created elements. This miracle, like others in the biblical narrative, serves a symbolic purpose, indicating Jesus's divine authority and pointing to the transformation he brings about in the lives of believers.

Miraculous Healings and Medical Science

The healing miracles of Jesus are of particular interest in light of modern medicine. When Jesus heals a leper (*Mark 1:40-42*), the immediate restoration of health contrasts sharply with the gradual process of healing understood by medical science. These healings are not meant to be viewed as alternative medical practices but as signs of the kingdom of Jehovah, wherein sickness and death will no longer have dominion (*Revelation 21:4*).

The Significance of Miracles in Ancient Context

It is essential to consider the function of miracles in their ancient context. Miracles served as a means for Jehovah to authenticate His messengers and their message (*Hebrews 2:3-4*). In a time and culture where supernatural events were more readily accepted as part of the human experience, miracles were a powerful tool in God's revelatory process.

The Purpose of Miracles in Divine Economy

Miracles had specific purposes in the biblical narrative: they confirmed the divine mission of Jehovah's messengers, provided a foretaste of the coming eschatological age, and vindicated the oppressed. They were never intended to be an ongoing method of divine operation but were limited to times of significant transition and revelation, such as the exodus, the prophetic era, and the coming of the Messiah.

Miracles and Faith

In the scientific age, miracles often come under scrutiny, and their relationship with faith is questioned. In the biblical perspective, miracles were not merely for the purpose of generating belief but for confirming the truth that was being proclaimed. Faith was a response to the revelation of Jehovah, not solely to the miraculous act itself (*John 20:29*).

Miracles and the Canon of Scripture

As the canon of Scripture was completed, the particular period of miracles, signs, and wonders as common occurrences in the life of the early church came to an end. The recorded miracles in Scripture serve as a testimony to Jehovah's dealings with humanity, providing a foundation for faith that does not depend on the continual display of miraculous events. The Scriptures themselves are presented as sufficient for instruction in faith and practice (*2 Timothy 3:16-17*).

Edward D. Andrews

Miracles in the Life of Believers Today

For believers today, the emphasis is on living in accordance with the Scriptures rather than seeking or expecting miraculous interventions. This does not negate Jehovah's capacity to act in extraordinary ways, but it does mean that such actions are not the normative experience for believers.

Understanding biblical miracles in a scientific age requires a nuanced approach that respects both the integrity of the biblical text and the insights of modern science. While the events described as miracles in the Bible are not repeatable or explainable by scientific methods, they remain a vital part of the biblical narrative, providing insight into Jehovah's character and purposes. In a world governed by natural laws, the biblical account of miracles invites believers to consider a reality that is not limited to what can be seen or measured but includes the sovereign work of Jehovah that surpasses human understanding.

The Scriptural Precedent: Miracles Transcending Physics

In the biblical narrative, miracles are extraordinary events that defy the laws of physics as we understand them. These events are not random or capricious but serve as a testament to the sovereign power of Jehovah and His purposes within the fabric of human history. They suspend or alter the regular functioning of the natural world, confirming the authority and message of those through whom they were performed. Such acts are not hidden within the texts but are placed at the forefront of God's interaction with His creation and His people.

Creation: The Inaugural Miracle

The inaugural miracle, the act of creation, establishes the precedent for all subsequent miracles. The Hebrew word for create, *bara* (בָּרָא), implies a divine act of bringing something into existence that did not exist before (*Genesis 1:1*). The creation of the universe, ex nihilo—out of nothing—is the foundational miracle from which all other supernatural acts derive their possibility. If Jehovah could call the cosmos into being, then altering the established order of that creation is certainly within His capability.

Miracles of Provision and Judgment in the Hebrew Scriptures

The Hebrew Scriptures are replete with instances where Jehovah intervenes in the natural order. For instance, when the Israelites are fed with manna from heaven (*Exodus 16*), the term *manna* (מָן) itself means "What is it?" This foodstuff, unlike any naturally occurring substance, appeared with the morning dew and ceased with the arrival in Canaan, a clear suspension of natural processes for a specific divine purpose.

Another profound example is the parting of the Red Sea, described in *Exodus 14*. Here, the word used for the sea's division, *baqa* (בָּקַע), denotes a forceful splitting, an act that interrupted the physical properties of water to allow an entire nation to pass through on dry ground—a phenomenon inexplicable by natural laws.

Miracles of Jesus in the Gospels

Moving to the New Testament, Jesus's miracles are not merely powerful deeds but signs (*semeia* - σημεῖα) that

119

indicate his unique relationship with Jehovah and His authority over creation. Take, for instance, the calming of the storm (*Mark 4:39*). The Greek term used here for "calm" is *siopao* (σιωπάω), implying a sudden cessation of noise. The immediate stillness of the sea defies meteorological explanation, showcasing Jesus's divine authority over nature.

In the miracle of Jesus walking on water (*Matthew 14:25*), the act itself transcends physical laws. The Greek term *peripateo* (περιπατέω) is typically used for walking on solid ground, yet here it is used for Jesus walking on the surface of the sea, indicating an action that is naturally impossible but is made possible by divine intervention.

The Resurrection: The Culminating Miracle

The resurrection of Jesus from the dead is the cornerstone of Christian faith and the ultimate miracle that transcends physical law. The Greek term for resurrection, *anastasis* (ἀνάστασις), means "rising up" or "standing up again." This event, described throughout the New Testament (*1 Corinthians 15*), validates Jesus's deity and is presented as a historical occurrence with theological significance that anchors Christian hope.

The Biblical View of Miracles and Modern Physics

From a biblical standpoint, miracles are not violations of the natural order but are instead instances where a higher order temporarily supersedes the usual physical laws. In every miraculous event, from healing the sick to raising the dead, the Scriptures present a consistent theme: Jehovah's power has dominion over all creation, and His purposes are fulfilled through both the ordinary and the extraordinary.

Understanding Miracles in the Context of God's Sovereignty

The biblical miracles teach that the natural order is not a closed system but is open to the will of Jehovah, who is both the author and sustainer of all that exists. Jehovah, who established the laws of nature, is not subject to them. Thus, when miracles occur, they are not acts of chaos but of re-creation and restoration, signaling the reality of Jehovah's kingdom breaking into the natural world.

Implications for Faith in a Scientific Age

In a world governed by an understanding of physics and predictable natural law, the biblical accounts of miracles challenge us to consider the role of divine agency and the limitations of human comprehension. The recognition of miracles does not necessitate a rejection of science; rather, it invites an acknowledgment that science describes the usual pattern of the world, while miracles point to the sovereign will of Jehovah that stands above those patterns.

The scriptural precedent of miracles transcending physics is foundational to the biblical narrative. While the occurrence of such events is historically confined to periods of revelatory significance, their impact is enduring, providing a witness to Jehovah's supreme power and divine purpose. As such, the biblical record of miracles is not simply a collection of ancient stories but a testimony to the enduring reality of Jehovah's intervention in the world He created, inviting believers to a faith that encompasses both the seen and the unseen, the natural and the supernatural.

Edward D. Andrews

CHAPTER 8 Overcoming Common Objections That Miracles Are Really Possible

Some Just Do Not Believe

In discussing the plausibility of miracles, a significant hurdle is the skepticism that pervades much of modern thought. Disbelief in miracles often stems from various sources—scientific mindsets, philosophical presuppositions, and at times a misunderstanding of what the Bible itself teaches about miracles. Addressing these objections requires a multifaceted approach, balancing respect for the disciplines of science and philosophy with a firm grounding in biblical doctrine.

The Challenge of Scientism

One prevalent objection to the possibility of miracles arises from the perspective of scientism—the belief that science is the ultimate path to knowledge and that anything outside its purview cannot be true. This view posits that because miracles cannot be tested or replicated in a laboratory setting, they must be relegated to the realm of myth or superstition. However, this position fails to acknowledge that science, while immensely valuable, is inherently limited to studying repeatable phenomena in the natural world. Miracles, by definition, are singular acts of divine intervention and thus outside the scope of scientific inquiry.

Historical Reality versus Repeatable Phenomena

Critics often demand empirical evidence for miracles, expecting them to be verifiable in the same way as natural events. Yet the historical nature of biblical miracles means they are not subject to repetition or laboratory analysis. Their validation comes through the reliability of the historical records, such as those of Jesus's resurrection, which are corroborated by multiple eyewitness accounts (*1 Corinthians 15:3-8*). The Greek term *martys* (μάρτυς), meaning "witness," underscores the testimonial nature of the evidence for miracles.

The Assumption of Naturalism

Naturalism is the philosophical belief that everything arises from natural properties and causes, and supernatural or spiritual explanations are excluded or discounted. This worldview precludes miracles a priori, assuming that all events must have a natural cause. The issue with this standpoint is that it dismisses the possibility of miracles without examination, essentially ruling out any evidence for the supernatural. The Bible, however, asserts that Jehovah, who is not bound by the natural order He created, is capable of intervening in His creation (*Isaiah 45:18*).

Miracles and the Laws of Logic

Some skeptics argue that miracles are impossible because they violate the laws of logic. However, this misconception confuses the laws of nature with the laws of logic. The laws of logic, such as the law of non-contradiction, are fundamental principles of reason that govern the truth of statements, not physical events. A miracle does not entail a logical contradiction; it is not asserting that an event is both occurring and not occurring in the same manner at the same time. Rather, miracles are about the One who established the laws of nature having the authority to temporarily set them aside.

The Question of Divine Will

Many objections to miracles question why a divine being would choose to intervene in some instances and not others. The scriptural position is that miracles are not arbitrary but serve specific purposes in God's salvific plan. For example, the miracles surrounding Israel's exodus from Egypt were signs meant to demonstrate Jehovah's power over the false gods of Egypt and to deliver His people (*Exodus 7-12*). Similarly, the miracles performed by Jesus were not just displays of power but attestations to his identity as God's Anointed One, or Messiah (*Acts 2:22*).

The Role of Faith

At the heart of the disbelief in miracles is often a misunderstanding of the role of faith. Faith is not a blind leap into the unknown but a trust in the reliability of God and His Word. The Greek word for faith, *pistis* (πίστις), conveys a sense of trustworthiness and conviction. Biblical faith is not opposed to reason; rather, it goes beyond what reason can ascertain alone. It is through faith that believers accept the historical accounts of miracles, not as naive acceptance of the improbable, but as confidence in the trustworthy character of Jehovah, who has revealed Himself both in creation and in scripture.

Overcoming the common objections to the possibility of miracles requires an understanding that extends beyond the confines of empirical science and acknowledges the philosophical presuppositions that influence much of the skepticism. It also necessitates a proper interpretation of scripture, recognizing the context and purposes of miracles in the biblical narrative. By addressing these objections with both reason and faith, one can hold to the historicity and possibility of miracles as genuine acts of God that bear witness to His nature and purposes, as documented in the Bible.

Violation of the Laws of Nature

A common objection to the possibility of miracles is the assertion that they violate the established laws of nature. To address this critique, it is vital to explore the nature of these laws and the sovereignty of God as depicted in Scripture.

The Character of Natural Laws

Natural laws are descriptions of how matter and energy interact; they are consistent patterns observed in the natural world. However, these laws are not prescriptive but descriptive—they describe what happens under normal circumstances. From a biblical perspective, Jehovah, who established these laws at creation, retains authority over them.

Miracles and Sovereignty

When discussing the intersection of miracles and natural law, it's important to understand the concept of divine sovereignty. The Hebrew word *Adonai* (אֲדֹנָי) reflects Jehovah's sovereignty as the ultimate authority over the universe. The miracles described in the Bible are expressions of God's will, intervening in the natural order in a way that supersedes these laws without nullifying them.

Biblical Examples of Superseding Natural Laws

Scripture contains several instances where natural laws are superseded by divine action. One prominent example is Jesus walking on water (Matthew 14:25-26). The law of buoyancy dictates that humans cannot walk on water, yet this event demonstrates Jesus's authority over physical laws. Similarly, the resurrection of Lazarus (John 11:43-44) contradicts biological laws—once death occurs and decomposition sets in, life does not return. Yet, in this miraculous event, the power of Jehovah, channeled through Jesus, reverses death itself.

The Purpose of Miracles

Miracles serve specific purposes in the biblical narrative. They are signs pointing to deeper truths—signs meant to reveal God's character, affirm the authority of His messengers, and unfold His redemptive plan. The Greek term *semeion* (σημεῖον), often translated as "sign," conveys this purposeful aspect of miracles. They are not whimsical breaches of natural law but deliberate acts intended to draw attention to Jehovah's power and purposes.

The Red Sea Parting

Consider the parting of the Red Sea (Exodus 14:21-22), a defining miracle in Israel's history. The laws of fluid dynamics would predict the waters to continue their normal flow. Yet, in this miraculous event, the waters are held at bay, allowing the Israelites to pass. This act is not a random display of power but a sign of deliverance and a testament to the covenant relationship between Jehovah and His people.

Red Sea: A Passage of Faith and Power

In discussions about the great Exodus of the Israelites from Egypt, a contentious issue has been the nature of the *yam-suph'* which is commonly known as the "Red Sea." Contrary to suggestions that it refers to a "sea of reeds" and implies a marshy crossing, the ancient translators of the Greek Septuagint rendered it as *e·ry·thra' tha'las·sa*, or "Red Sea." This translation was carried into the writings of the New Testament, used by both Luke in Acts 7:36 and Paul in Hebrews 11:29. The apostle Paul further cements this understanding when he speaks of the Israelites being baptized into Moses "in the cloud and in the sea" (1 Corinthians 10:1-2), suggesting a literal, enveloping body of water and not a shallow marsh.

The miraculous crossing of the Red Sea is no small feat. Scripture describes the waters as being parted, creating walls on either side of the Israelites as they crossed on dry ground. This was no shallow wade but a path through a depth significant enough to later swallow up the Egyptian pursuers as if they had plunged into the depths like stone (Exodus 15:5). The event signifies not merely a geographical relocation but a spiritual transformation, symbolizing baptism into a new covenantal life under Moses' leadership.

Route of the Exodus and the Egyptian Capital

The route of the Exodus is intricately linked to the location of the Egyptian capital and the crossing site. Memphis is traditionally considered the capital during this period, suggesting the Israelites began their exodus nearby, enabling Moses to meet Pharaoh and later lead the Israelites out of Rameses towards Succoth within the allotted time frame (Exodus 12:29-42). This timeline discounts the possibility of a northern route through the Wadi Tumilat, as it would be too far from Memphis to be feasible.

Early commentators suggested routes familiar to pilgrims, such as the el Haj route from Cairo to Suez. However, after reaching Etham "at the edge of the wilderness," God's instruction to Moses to encamp before Pihahiroth indicated a strategic move that would appear confusing to Pharaoh (Exodus 14:1-3). The Hebrew verb for "turn back" suggests not a mere detour but a significant change in direction, possibly leading the Israelites to the east of Jebel ʿAtaqah. This positioning would effectively trap them, necessitating a miraculous intervention for escape.

The Miracle at the Sea

The crossing site, then, needed to be sufficiently distant from the Gulf of Suez to prevent Pharaoh's forces from simply going around the water to reach the Israelites. Instead, the Egyptians were led to pursue them into the sea bed itself (Exodus 14:22-23). The cloud that moved behind the Israelites served as a barrier of darkness to the Egyptians while providing light to the Israelites, demonstrating God's protective presence (Exodus 14:19-20).

Width and Depth of the Crossing

Considering the number of Israelites and their livestock, the path through the sea was likely quite wide, allowing them to cross in battle formation without panic. This formation would have extended several kilometers, enabling them to cross within the night.

The Confusion and Destruction of the Egyptians

When the Egyptians pursued, they found themselves in chaos, with their chariots becoming bogged down. Jehovah's intervention was clear as He threw the Egyptian forces into disarray during the early morning hours, causing their ultimate destruction as the waters returned (Exodus 14:24-28).

Waters "Congealed"

The Bible uses the term "congealed" to describe the waters during the crossing (Exodus 15:8). This term does not necessarily imply freezing but rather suggests a consistency that could hold the waters like walls. This phenomenon was a divine act, transcending natural explanation, as no visible force was sustaining these towering walls of water.

A Testimony of Deliverance

The escape across the Red Sea was complete when the Israelites reached the eastern shore, and the waters returned to their place, covering the Egyptian forces. This event stood as a testament to God's promise and power, as Moses had declared: "The Egyptians whom you do see today you will not see again, no, never again" (Exodus 14:13).

The parting of the Red Sea stands as an enduring testimony to Jehovah's ability to save His people, illustrating His dominion over the forces of nature and the affairs of nations. For the Israelites, it was a defining moment of deliverance, a sign of their unique covenant with Jehovah, and a prelude to the giving of the Law at Sinai. The crossing of the Red Sea, therefore, is not just a historical or geographical event but a foundational narrative of faith, revealing God's character and His commitment to His people's liberation and guidance.

Miracles as Foretastes of Future Reality

Miracles also provide a glimpse into the future kingdom where the effects of sin and the curse are reversed. The healing miracles of Jesus, for instance, offer a foretaste of the future resurrection where "there will be no more death" (Revelation 21:4). Such miracles temporarily suspend the laws of entropy and decay to point towards this promised restoration.

The Logical Coherence of Miracles

The logical coherence of miracles within the biblical worldview must be maintained. A miracle does not imply that God is capricious or that He violates His nature. Instead, miracles demonstrate that the laws of nature are subject to the will of Jehovah. They are exceptional, not because they are illogical, but because they manifest the power of God in ways that surpass our normal experience.

Miracles in the Context of Faith

Understanding miracles within the context of faith does not negate the importance of the laws of nature but places these laws in the proper perspective as part of the created order under divine authority. Believers are called not to a blind acceptance of impossibilities but to a reasoned faith in Jehovah's power and will to act beyond the ordinary operations of nature when it serves His purpose.

The objection that miracles violate the laws of nature assumes that these laws are inviolable and autonomous. However, from the standpoint of biblical theology, these laws operate under the sovereignty of Jehovah. Miracles, therefore, are not violations but are instances where God, for His purposes, chooses to act in a manner that supersedes the regular patterns of the natural world. These acts are signs meant to reveal His character, demonstrate His covenant faithfulness, and point to the ultimate redemption and restoration of all things.

Fake Miracles Does Not Mean No Miracles

In addressing the skepticism towards miracles based on the existence of counterfeit miracles, it is critical to establish a clear distinction between the authentic acts of Jehovah as recorded in Scripture and the deceptive acts that masquerade as divine.

Deceptive Practices in Ancient Times

The Scriptures themselves warn about false prophets performing signs and wonders. For example, in Deuteronomy 13:1-3, Moses cautions against prophets who perform *oth* (אוֹת, "sign") or *mopheth* (מוֹפֵת, "wonder") to lead people astray. The presence of such deception does not negate the reality of genuine miracles but rather affirms the necessity of discernment.

The Magicians of Pharaoh's Court

A profound biblical illustration is found in the confrontation between Moses and the magicians of Pharaoh's court (Exodus 7:11-12). The Egyptian magicians replicated some of the miraculous signs that Jehovah performed through Moses and Aaron, such as turning staffs into serpents. Yet, Aaron's staff, representative of Jehovah's power, swallowed up the magicians' staffs, symbolizing the superiority of true divine power over deceitful imitation.

New Testament Warnings

The New Testament continues this theme with warnings about false Christs and false prophets performing *pseudos* (ψεῦδος, "false") miracles. Jesus himself said that false prophets would arise and perform great signs and wonders to deceive, if possible, even the elect (Matthew 24:24). The existence of these false wonders does not diminish the reality of true miracles but emphasizes the need for vigilance and a return to the Scriptures for verification.

Miracles as a Testimony

Authentic miracles in the Bible serve as a testimony to God's revelation. They are not merely acts of power but carry a message. For instance, the miracles performed by Jesus, such as the healing of the man with the withered hand (Luke 6:6-10), were not just displays of power but demonstrations of divine compassion and Sabbath truths.

Discerning the Source

In discerning the source of a miracle, one must look to its alignment with Scripture. True miracles will harmonize with Jehovah's purposes and character. In Acts, the apostle Peter healed a man lame from birth (Acts 3:6-8), an act that led to the glorification of God and the spread of the gospel. The source of a miracle, therefore, must be tested by its fruits—does it glorify Jehovah, and is it consistent with His revealed will?

The Role of Miracles

Understanding the role of miracles in biblical times also aids in discerning their authenticity. Initially, miracles played a pivotal role in establishing the foundations of faith and were particularly prevalent during times when new revelations were given. As the canon of Scripture was completed, the role of such overt miracles diminished. This transition does not negate the occurrence of miracles but contextualizes their primary purpose in redemptive history.

The presence of counterfeit miracles should not lead to the wholesale dismissal of all miracles. Rather, it should prompt a careful and scriptural examination of the claims of miraculous occurrences. In the Bible, miracles by Jehovah had a clear purpose, a divine message, and led to the uplifting of true worship. Counterfeits, while they exist, do not invalidate the reality of divine power but serve as a reminder of the need for discernment grounded in a sound understanding of God's Word.

Miracles Only in Times of Ignorance

A common objection to the possibility of miracles today is the assertion that they were exclusive to "times of ignorance," when ancient peoples lacked scientific understanding and thus attributed inexplicable phenomena to divine intervention. This perspective posits that as human knowledge and science progressed, the need for and incidence of miracles waned.

The Role of Miracles in Antiquity

Miracles in the Bible served as signs pointing beyond themselves to a divine message or truth. In ancient times, when literacy rates were low, and scientific understanding was in its infancy, miracles functioned as vivid, powerful affirmations of Jehovah's sovereignty and as confirmations of His messengers' authority. For instance, the ten plagues on Egypt culminating in the parting of the Red Sea (*Yam-Suf*, יַם־סוּף) displayed Jehovah's dominion over the natural world and his supremacy over the Egyptian gods.

Miracles as Signs for Believers and Unbelievers

Miracles were not merely for those who lacked scientific acumen but also for the express purpose of revelation and validation of Jehovah's servants. In John's Gospel, Jesus performed a miracle at Cana, turning water into wine (*hudor eis oinon*, ὕδωρ εἰς οἶνον), which is described as the first of the signs through which he revealed his glory, and his disciples believed in him (John 2:11).

A Sign for All Times

Paul, in his address on Mars Hill (*Areios Pagos*, Ἄρειος Πάγος), spoke to educated Greeks about Jehovah, referencing the "times of ignorance" that God overlooked but now commands all people everywhere to repent (Acts 17:30). Paul does not dismiss the miracles of the past as products of ignorance but uses them to build a case for a knowledgeable faith.

Scientific Knowledge and Divine Power

The advance of scientific knowledge does not preclude the occurrence of miracles. Rather than being an argument against miracles, increased knowledge can enhance appreciation for the wonders of Jehovah's creation and for any extraordinary acts that transcend natural law. Scientific understanding helps to distinguish between natural processes and miraculous events.

Scriptural Examples

The miracles recorded in the Scriptures do not depict a deity operating in the shadows of human ignorance but one who is sovereign over all creation. The resurrection of Jesus (anastasis, ἀνάστασις) is a cornerstone event that defies natural explanation, serving as the ultimate validation of Jesus's divine mission and authority. It is an event that has stood the scrutiny of both ancient and modern inquiry.

Miracles in the Context of Divine Revelation

In biblical history, miracles often occurred at key junctures of divine revelation: the giving of the Law, the ministries of Elijah and Elisha during a time of great apostasy, and the life and ministry of Jesus and the apostles as the Christian congregation was being established. The miracles served as beacons of truth, not concessions to ignorance.

The Closing of the Canon

The completion of the biblical canon did bring a kind of closure to the era of widespread, overt miraculous events. The written Word became the primary means by which Jehovah communicates His will to humankind. While this shift occurred, it does not suggest that Jehovah's ability or willingness to perform miracles ceased but that the primary method of revealing divine will became the Scriptures.

Miracles and Faith Today

While the frequency and purpose of miracles have shifted, this does not mean miracles are impossible in modern times. They remain within Jehovah's power and prerogative. However, the biblical record suggests that instead of expecting regular miraculous interventions, faith should now rest on the sure foundation of God's Word.

The assertion that miracles are a feature of "times of ignorance" fails to recognize their role as divine signs that accompanied pivotal moments in redemptive history. While scientific progress has provided natural explanations for many phenomena once deemed miraculous, it has not eliminated the possibility of genuine miracles occurring according to Jehovah's purpose and timing. Faith is no longer founded on the expectation of miracles but is sustained by the truths revealed in the completed Scriptures.

The Best Attested Miracle

In discussing the best attested miracle within the Christian tradition, the resurrection of Jesus Christ stands as the paramount example. This event is not merely a single narrative among many but is the cornerstone upon which Christian faith is established. It is described in multiple independent sources within the New Testament and has been the focus of exhaustive scholarly scrutiny over the centuries.

Multiple Independent Attestations

The accounts of Jesus's resurrection appear in all four Gospels — Matthew, Mark, Luke, and John — which were written by different authors in different locales. Paul, whose letters are among the earliest Christian writings, refers to the resurrection in multiple passages, most notably in 1 Corinthians 15, where he emphasizes the resurrection as the critical element of the gospel. This event's attestation from multiple sources provides a strong historical foundation.

The Nature of the Resurrection Accounts

The Gospels present the resurrection as a historical event that was experienced by eyewitnesses. These accounts include details that argue against the resurrection being a legend or myth. For example, women are listed as the first witnesses to the empty tomb, which is significant because in the cultural context of the time, a woman's testimony was not highly valued. This is an example of the criterion of embarrassment in historical analysis, which suggests that such a detail would likely not be included if it were not true.

Post-Resurrection Appearances

The appearances of the resurrected Jesus (*Iesous anestē*, Ἰησοῦς ἀνέστη) are detailed in various contexts: to individuals like Mary Magdalene, to the disciples, and to larger groups, including an appearance to more than five hundred people at once (1 Corinthians 15:6). These appearances are presented as physical, tangible interactions where Jesus was seen and touched, and even ate with his disciples, providing a multidimensional attestation to the reality of the event.

Transformation of the Disciples

The disciples' transformation from despairing followers who abandoned Jesus at his arrest to bold proclaimers of his resurrection is a testament to the event's authenticity. The disciples claimed to have seen the risen Lord and their subsequent willingness to suffer persecution and death for this belief adds weight to their testimony. This is often cited as the criterion of dissimilarity — their actions were distinctly different before and after the event they described.

Extra-Biblical References

While the primary sources for the resurrection are within the New Testament, early Christian writings outside the biblical canon also reference the event, indicating that the resurrection narrative was established and widespread within early Christian communities. These writings do not serve as independent confirmation but demonstrate the centrality and uniformity of the resurrection belief among early Christians.

Theological Significance

Theologically, the resurrection is foundational to Christian doctrine. Paul states that if Christ has not been raised, then Christian preaching is in vain and faith is futile (1 Corinthians 15:14). The resurrection is seen as the validation of Jesus's life, teachings, and sacrificial death, and as Jehovah's powerful declaration of Jesus as the Messiah and Son of God.

Skeptical Challenges

Skeptics have proposed various naturalistic explanations for the resurrection accounts, such as the disciples experiencing hallucinations or the body of Jesus being stolen. However, these theories struggle to account for the wide variety of experiences and the consistency of the disciples' transformation and the growth of the early church.

The Role of Faith and History

While historical analysis can establish the plausibility of the resurrection, faith plays a role in accepting it as a miraculous event. The resurrection transcends the natural order and, as such, cannot be proven by historical methods alone. However, the historical evidence can bolster faith by showing that belief in the resurrection is not blind faith but is based on a substantial historical foundation.

The resurrection of Jesus is the best attested miracle in the Christian faith, with multiple, independent sources within the New Testament and additional early Christian writings. It is an event that has shaped history and has been the focal point of Christian belief since the first century.

While the physical miracles of Jesus's ministry, such as healings and exorcisms, were signs of his divine authority and compassion, the resurrection serves as the ultimate sign, attesting to Jesus's identity as the Messiah and to Jehovah's power to conquer death itself. The historical grounding of this event provides a compelling case for its reality, and it remains central to Christian faith and hope.

The Empty Tomb and the Report of the Guard

Eyewitnesses to the Resurrected Jesus

Miracles Are a Reality

CHAPTER 9 Unveiling Biblical Clues: The Secret Behind the Egyptian Pyramids' Creation

The Deluge and Human Longevity

Tracing the Post-Flood Decline in Age and Its Impact on Human Development

The global Flood, described in the book of Genesis, presents a pivotal moment in human history. As the deluge waters receded, the antediluvian world, known for its remarkable longevity and intellectual prowess, gave way to a new epoch marked by a steady decline in human lifespan. This transformation held profound implications for the subsequent trajectory of human development and civilization building, potentially including the construction of ancient monuments such as the Egyptian pyramids.

The Antediluvian World: A Portrait of Longevity and Wisdom

In the antediluvian period, Scripture recounts lives extending nearly a millennium. Adam lived for 930 years, Seth for 912, and Methuselah reached an unparalleled 969 years (Genesis 5:5, 8, 27). Such expansive lifespans would have allowed for an accumulation of wisdom and knowledge. Imagine a mind, not dulled by age as we know it, growing only in acuity and scope over centuries. The

141

original Hebrew word for "man" is אדם (*'adam*), connecting humanity directly to the earth from which we were formed, highlighting a creation designed for robustness and endurance.

Post-Diluvian Reality: A Sudden Shift in Human Vitality

However, after the floodwaters subsided, we observe a drastic reduction in human lifespans. Noah, a preacher of righteousness who lived 950 years, witnessed this decline firsthand as his descendants lived progressively shorter lives (Genesis 9:29). His son Shem, for example, lived 600 years—a significant decrease, yet still far beyond what we would consider a full life today (Genesis 11:10-11). This change implies not only altered physical conditions but also a potential decrease in the vigor necessary to sustain such extended lifespans.

The term for life or living in Hebrew is חַי (*chai*), a concept that encompasses more than mere biological existence; it implies vitality and dynamism. The post-flood decrease in longevity, therefore, points to a diminished *chai*, a contraction of life's robust vitality.

Cognitive Echoes of a Nearly Perfect Intellect

Despite the reduced lifespans, the immediate post-diluvian generations still possessed lifespans that greatly exceed our own, suggesting that they retained vestiges of antediluvian intellect and capability. This can be seen in the efforts of men like Nimrod, a great-grandson of Noah. Nimrod, as noted in Genesis 10:8-10, established the first kingdom on earth after the Flood and was considered a mighty one on the earth, a master of survival and civilization building. The Hebrew גִּבּוֹר (*gibbor*) associated with Nimrod, signifies strength, not merely physical but in leadership and innovation.

The Diminishing of Lifespan and Its Cultural Ramifications

The gradual reduction in human longevity had significant ramifications for the transmission of knowledge and culture. As lifespans decreased, so did the window for learning and passing on knowledge. In the antediluvian world, centuries of personal growth and learning could be directly transmitted; post-flood, the oral tradition would have had to suffice for the dissemination of this knowledge before it waned or was lost entirely.

Technological and Architectural Mastery Post-Flood

Even with diminishing lifespans, the post-diluvian world demonstrated remarkable feats of engineering and construction. This is exemplified by the city of Babel and its tower, an endeavor so audacious that it led to Jehovah's intervention, confounding their language and scattering them across the earth (Genesis 11:1-9). The word בָּלַל (*balal*), meaning to jumble or confuse, describes the divine action at Babel, illustrating the immediate hindrance to collective human effort.

Dispersion to Egypt: Retaining the Echoes of Edenic Genius

As people dispersed from Babel to regions like Egypt, they carried with them the remnants of their antediluvian heritage. This included not only their shortened yet still considerable lifespans but the cumulative knowledge of generations. The Egyptian pyramids, standing as a testament to human ingenuity, could very well embody this residual Edenic brilliance. The intelligence required to conceptualize and construct such monumental edifices suggests a level of sophistication that may have its roots in the wisdom handed down from a world before the Flood.

Contemplating Post-Flood Ingenuity in the Face of Declining Age

When comparing the intellectual capacity of those like Abraham and his contemporaries to modern geniuses such as Albert Einstein, we must consider the impact of longevity on knowledge and experience. Though Einstein's 76 years produced groundbreaking insights into the nature of reality, imagine the potential intellectual achievements of individuals whose lives spanned centuries and who were closer to the cognitive perfection of Eden.

In conclusion, the deluge's impact on human longevity marked a turning point in the development of post-flood civilizations. While human lifespans shortened dramatically, the initial post-diluvian generations still exhibited remarkable cognitive abilities, possibly contributing to the construction of enigmatic structures like the Egyptian pyramids. These achievements offer a glimpse into a world that, while separated from us by time and lifespan, shares a common lineage of divine creation and human ingenuity.

Intelligence in Perfection: Unpacking the Cognitive Might of Pre-Flood Humanity

The narrative of pre-Flood humanity, as chronicled in the Hebrew Scriptures, offers a profound window into the capabilities and intellectual potential of early mankind. Delving into the antediluvian epoch, we uncover a human experience starkly different from our contemporary condition, particularly in terms of cognitive capacity and lifespan. The pre-Flood era, marked by near-millennial lifespans, fostered an environment where knowledge could accumulate at a staggering pace, potentially leading to intellectual heights that modernity has yet to scale.

Antediluvian Longevity: A Conduit for Cognitive Expansion

The patriarchs of Genesis lived to ages that would today be considered mythological. Adam, for instance, lived 930 years (Genesis 5:5), and Methuselah reached 969 years (Genesis 5:27). It's not merely the number of years that captivates, but the implications these extended years have on cognitive retention and knowledge acquisition. The Hebrew term יָמִים (*yamim*, days or years) denotes not just the passage of time but the fullness thereof—years replete with experiences and learnings.

Longevity afforded the antediluvian minds an unparalleled continuity of thought and wisdom. Imagine a scholar today, enriched by 900 years of continual learning, unimpeded by the decline of old age as we know it. The cognitive potential would be nothing short of astounding. The Hebrew Scriptures imply that the pre-Flood human brain, unmarred by the genetic bottleneck and environmental stresses that would follow, operated at a caliber close to the original design of perfection.

Cognitive Excellence in Edenic Proximity

Those earliest descendants of Adam and Eve were, according to Scripture, only a few generational steps from the perfection of Eden. דַּעַת (*da'at*, knowledge), a significant term in Hebrew, encompasses understanding, wisdom, and skill. With this in mind, we can extrapolate that antediluvian knowledge wasn't merely factual recall but also included profound understanding and skillfulness in applying what was known to manipulate and master the environment.

We can glean from the Genesis account that humans were not idle in their intellectual endeavors. Cain's descendant, Tubal-cain, was a "forger of all instruments of bronze and iron" (Genesis 4:22), a clear indication of sophisticated knowledge in metallurgy. Jabal, another of Cain's lineage, is known as the "father of such as dwell in tents, and of such as have cattle" (Genesis 4:20), suggesting a nuanced understanding of domestication and pastoral life.

From Oral Tradition to Monumental Construction

The oral tradition of pre-Flood humanity would have been a robust conduit for transmitting vast stores of knowledge. Without written records, the longevity of life itself became the medium for preserving and sharing wisdom. Such an unbroken chain of oral transmission, when combined with remarkable cognitive abilities, may well have laid the foundation for feats of architecture and engineering that outpaced anything seen in subsequent ages, at least until the modern era.

As the dispersed descendants of Babel journeyed to regions like Egypt, they carried with them this extraordinary cognitive inheritance. It is reasonable to postulate that these early post-Babel builders, still benefitting from the waning echoes of Edenic intelligence, possessed the know-how to construct the towering pyramids of Egypt. It is within the realm of possibility that their methodologies, now lost to time, were rooted in principles and practices handed down from a pre-Flood world.

The Nimrod Paradigm: Insight into Post-Diluvian Ingenuity

Nimrod, a mighty hunter *before* Jehovah (Genesis 10:9), where לִפְנֵי (*liph'nei*) connotes a sense of presence and perhaps opposition, stands as a testament to the residual might of antediluvian intellect. Nimrod's reputation and exploits, likely enhanced by his proximity to the cognitive zenith of humanity, suggest that his empire-building was fueled by wisdom and understanding that exceeded the norm even for his time.

Post-Babel Intellectual Dispersion

The division of languages at Babel (Genesis 11:1-9) presents a pivotal moment in human intellectual history. The dispersion of people with their unique tongues carried the seeds of diverse cultures and thought systems. Yet, even fragmented, the underlying cognitive prowess these groups possessed, as they settled in regions like Egypt, cannot be understated. Their lifespans, though shortened, remained impressive by our standards, indicating that the decline from antediluvian longevity was gradual.

Contemplating the Pyramid Builders: A Cognitive Legacy

Considering the pyramids' construction during a time when lifespans, though reduced, still far exceeded today's standards, it becomes plausible to conjecture that the builders were leveraging a composite wisdom accrued over centuries. Just as Albert Einstein's brilliance shone through within the brief span of 76 years, how much more could have been achieved by minds nearly perfect in form, honed by centuries of learning and experience?

As such, when we marvel at the Egyptian pyramids, we may well be admiring the vestiges of a cognitive might once common to humanity. The precise alignment, the astronomical knowledge embedded in their placement, and the engineering prowess that has perplexed modern scholars may all be echoes of an intellectual capacity that was once a defining characteristic of human existence.

In the pursuit of understanding the Egyptian pyramids, it is thus essential to consider them not merely as structures of stone but as monuments to the human mind's potential in its most pristine state—a potential closely aligned with the divine image, rich in knowledge, understanding, and the application thereof, as presented in the Biblical narrative.

Craftsmanship in Genesis

Early Innovations from the Lineage of Cain

The narrative of Genesis unfolds with profound subtleties that reveal not just the spiritual but also the material progression of early human society. This progression is nowhere more evident than in the record of Cain's lineage, where the Bible details the embryonic stages of human innovation and craftsmanship, setting a precedent that would echo through the halls of history to the very stones of the Egyptian pyramids.

The Genesis of Craftsmanship and Urban Development

After his fateful crime, Cain departed from the presence of Jehovah and settled in the land of Nod, east of Eden. It was there that Cain "engaged in building a city," a task necessitating considerable organizational skill and the beginning of urban planning (Genesis 4:16-17). This endeavor marked a significant departure from the pastoral life described previously in Genesis, indicating a shift towards sedentism and complex social structures.

Cain's efforts imply a level of architectural knowledge that may seem advanced for the period. The undertaking of city-building suggests that Cain, and by extension, his contemporaries and descendants, possessed practical abilities in structuring their environment—a foreshadowing of the imposing edifices like the pyramids, which similarly demanded expertise in organization, administration, and labor management.

The Diversification of Human Vocation

The diversification of human vocation is starkly illustrated in the lineage of Cain. Jabal, for instance, is cited as "the founder of those who dwell in tents and have livestock" (Genesis 4:20), highlighting a pastoral lifestyle that contrasts with Cain's urban inclination. Here, we find the inception of animal husbandry and the nomadic lifestyle, the mastery of which would require extensive knowledge of animal behavior, genetics, and ecology.

In the same breath, the Bible mentions Jubal, "the father of all those who play the harp and flute" (Genesis 4:21), signifying the origins of music and arts. The creation and utilization of musical instruments denote a sophisticated understanding of acoustics and craftsmanship, and Jubal's designation as a "father" implies he was a pioneer, an inventor, an inspirer of culture.

The Birth of Metallurgy

More pertinent to the subject of Egyptian pyramids is Tubal-Cain, "a forger of every sort of tool of copper and iron" (Genesis 4:22). This reference is the first mention of metallurgy in the Bible, indicating a considerable advance in technology. The ability to manipulate metals would have profound implications for tool-making, construction, and eventually, the development of techniques necessary for monumental architecture. This was the genesis of a skill set that would enable humanity to erect structures of astonishing complexity and durability, like the pyramids, which still stand as a testament to such craftsmanship.

The advancements in metallurgy imply a comprehensive understanding of geology, chemistry, and the physics of heat and materials, which speaks to a much more sophisticated intellectual capacity than commonly attributed to ancient peoples. Tubal-Cain's work with metals laid the groundwork for the technological strides that were to come.

Intellectual Capacity and Lifespan

These early biblical figures were not just innovators; they were also individuals with lifespans reaching into the hundreds of years. Their longevity, coupled with a mental acuity perhaps diminished from but still closely resembling that of their almost perfect forebears, would have afforded them an incredible capacity for cumulative knowledge. This knowledge was passed down through oral tradition, allowing for an accumulation of wisdom and understanding that far exceeds modern post-industrial revolution education systems.

With such long lives, these individuals would have had centuries to refine their techniques, experiment with new methods, and pass on complex information. This intergenerational transfer of knowledge, enhanced by their extended lifespans, would have accelerated the pace of technological and cultural development.

The Shadow of Perfection in a Fallen World

The Scripture subtly underscores the inherent potential of mankind, created in the image of God, to reach impressive heights of creativity and innovation, even in a fallen state. The intellectual and creative capabilities demonstrated by the lineage of Cain are a testament to this. Jehovah created mankind with the ability to shape their environment, to innovate, to create tools and art, and to build societies of significant complexity.

The Echoes of Antediluvian Brilliance in the Pyramids

Fast forwarding to the era of the pyramids, the echoes of this antediluvian brilliance are undeniable. Those early post-flood generations, such as those during Abraham's time, would have retained much of this profound knowledge and intellectual vigor. It is reasonable, then, to postulate that the expertise displayed in the construction of the pyramids—the precise engineering, the astronomical alignments, and the sheer ambition of these projects—was a legacy of the intellectual and technical prowess honed over centuries by those whose lifespans and mental faculties approached the zenith of human potential.

The Legacy of Babel: Scattering of Skills and Knowledge

The dispersion at Babel scattered the families and their unique linguistic groups across the face of the earth. Each family carried with it a fragment of the collective knowledge amassed over the centuries. As they spread into regions like Egypt, they took their artisanal skills, their architectural expertise, and their crafts with them, seeding the knowledge that would culminate in the construction of the pyramids.

When considering the building of the Egyptian pyramids, it is essential to recognize the antediluvian and post-diluvian lineage of Cain as the cradle of human craftsmanship and intellectual prowess. The Bible, through its account of Cain's descendants, provides a window into the early advancements that likely served as a foundation for the innovations required to construct such ancient architectural marvels. These individuals, with lifespans that dwarf our own and intellects sharpened by near-perfect beginnings, embody the zenith of human potential—a potential that would find its expression in the stones of

Giza, standing as an enduring enigma and a silent testament to the craftsmanship detailed in Genesis.

Post-Diluvian Persistence: Carrying Forward the Craft in the Days of Abraham

The era immediately following the Great Flood, known as the post-diluvian period, was one of rapid human expansion and profound cultural development. As the descendants of Noah populated the earth, they bore with them the intellectual and technical prowess that had been cultivated across generations, a bridge between the antediluvian and the new world that emerged. In the days of Abraham, this persistence of skill and knowledge was evident in various forms, not the least of which is suggested by the construction of the Egyptian pyramids—a marvel of human ingenuity and perhaps a vestige of Edenic legacy.

The Continuity of Craftsmanship and Knowledge

In the shadow of Babel, with its hubris and resultant confusion of tongues (*balal* in Hebrew), the families dispersed, carrying not only their distinct languages but also their cumulative technological and architectural wisdom. The pyramids of Egypt, arising during the epoch of Abraham, serve as concrete examples of this advanced knowledge being applied. The meticulous engineering, astronomical alignment, and mathematical precision of these structures indicate that their builders possessed a profound understanding, which may well trace back to pre-Flood human capacities.

The legacy of Cain's lineage, with artisans like Tubal-Cain, who forged tools of copper and iron (*nechosheth* and *barzel* in Hebrew), suggests that metalworking and other crafts did not cease with the Deluge but rather were preserved through Noah and his descendants. Although the

Scripture does not provide exhaustive technical details, the longevity of post-diluvian patriarchs like Shem, who overlapped with Abraham for 150 years, implies a sustained transmission of knowledge through oral tradition. The Bible indicates that Shem was an immediate descendent of Noah and lived for many centuries, thus becoming a living repository of antediluvian knowledge, which he could have passed down.

Abraham's Era: A Convergence of Knowledge

Abraham's lifetime, according to biblical chronology, places him in a unique position during this unfolding of human expansion. Abraham himself, hailing from Ur of the Chaldeans, would have been privy to the rich cultural and intellectual milieu of his time. His own family would have been carriers of the knowledge that proliferated in the post-Babel world.

The Egyptian pyramids, constructed during the period surrounding Abraham's lifetime, stand as testaments to the complex skill sets that persisted from the antediluvian period. It is worth contemplating that these achievements were not merely the result of trial and error or simple empirical knowledge but were likely underpinned by sophisticated understanding handed down through generations, possibly originating from those early humans who were "closer to perfection."

Intellectual Capacity and Longevity: A Correlation

The intellectual acumen required to conceptualize and execute projects such as the pyramids is not to be understated. While the Bible does not explicitly link the construction of the pyramids to the descendants of Noah, it does offer insights into the correlation between the early post-diluvian human capacities and their extended lifespans.

Minds closer to perfection, as in the case of antediluvian patriarchs, would have a greater ability to accumulate and apply complex knowledge over their extended lifetimes.

In this light, Abraham and his contemporaries, though living shorter lives than their antediluvian ancestors, would still have benefitted from this accumulated wealth of knowledge. Their intellectual capabilities, though diminished compared to their antediluvian counterparts, were nonetheless extraordinary by our standards.

Technological Ingenuity in Post-Diluvian Context

The construction of the pyramids required not just architectural and mathematical expertise but also the development and application of advanced technologies. The forging of tools and the transportation of massive stones across vast distances involve a level of technological ingenuity that could not have sprung ex nihilo. It necessitated a background of accumulated knowledge, likely preserved through the oral traditions and practices of post-diluvian patriarchs.

The Role of Divine Providence in Human Skill

While human skill and intelligence were critical in post-diluvian advancements, it is important to consider the role of divine providence in this narrative. The dispersion at Babel, although an act of judgment, was also a mechanism for the diversification and development of human culture. Jehovah, in allowing mankind to spread across the earth, facilitated the proliferation of human knowledge and skill.

It is within this framework that we can appreciate the construction of the pyramids. While the Bible does not credit divine inspiration for their creation, it does acknowledge the capabilities bestowed upon humanity.

These capabilities, while impaired by sin, were nonetheless significant and, when guided by divine principles, could achieve remarkable outcomes.

Nimrod's Rebellion

Understanding the Ambition of the First Post-Flood Tyrant

In the aftermath of the great deluge, as chronicled in the book of Genesis, humanity began a new chapter under the sons of Noah: Shem, Ham, and Japheth. From these lines emerged various leaders, but one figure stands out with a reputation that echoed through the ancient narratives— Nimrod. *His legacy is etched in the annals of Biblical history*, not as a beacon of virtue, but as an emblem of human rebellion and pride.

The Genesis Account

The Genesis narrative introduces Nimrod in chapter 10, noting him as a *gibbor* (mighty one) on the earth. This term *gibbor* (גִּבּוֹר) often connotes a warrior or a person of great stature and prowess. He is further described as a *gibbor tsayid* (mighty hunter) before Jehovah. This title implies not only skill in hunting but also suggests an undertone of dominance and possibly even aggression toward others and toward God's order.

The Linguistic Nuance

The preposition *liph·neh'* (לִפְנֵי), translated as "before," can bear the connotation of "in front of" or "in the face of," indicating proximity. However, contextually, it can also imply opposition or defiance. This subtle yet significant linguistic detail hints at Nimrod's posture toward the divine authority. His actions were not merely independent of

Jehovah but were an affront to Him—a direct challenge to His sovereignty.

Nimrod's Empire

Nimrod's kingdom, as outlined in Genesis 10:10, commenced in Babel, Erech, Accad, and Calneh, in the land of Shinar (שִׁנְעָר). Shinar, identified with Sumer, was a region rich in cultural and technological innovation, which later became known as Babylonia. This setting provided fertile ground for Nimrod's ambitions, suggesting he leveraged the post-diluvian advancements for his empire-building.

The Spirit of Babel

The spirit of Babel, associated with Nimrod's reign, was one of collective human pride and defiance. The people's desire to construct a city and a tower whose top would reach the heavens was not just an architectural endeavor but a symbolic act of establishing a name for themselves, independent of Jehovah's will. This *ziggurat*, often perceived as the Tower of Babel, was a stairway to heaven in their eyes, but a monument to disobedience in scriptural terms.

Divine Response to Human Arrogance

Jehovah's intervention at Babel, by confounding the languages, was not merely to halt a construction project but to disperse a unified human effort that was veering away from divine purposes. The sudden fragmentation of language groups created barriers that led to the cessation of the project and scattered humanity across the globe, seeding the diversity of cultures and civilizations.

The Intellectual Legacy of the Antediluvian World

Nimrod, likely having been brought up with the antediluvian knowledge passed down through generations, would have possessed *considerable understanding*, perhaps touching upon what moderns would deem advanced. This wisdom, coupled with his ambition, would have been a formidable force. *It is within this context that some historians and theologians speculate on the potential connection between Nimrod's realm and the later construction of the Egyptian pyramids.*

The Egyptian Connection

While the Bible does not explicitly link Nimrod to the pyramids of Egypt, the migration of peoples from Shinar could have carried forth the knowledge and skills acquired under his rule. The technological and architectural prowess necessary for the pyramids might find a lineage back to the innovations sparked by figures like Nimrod.

Concluding Reflections on Nimrod's Ambition

Nimrod's story serves as a cautionary tale, illustrating the consequences of human pride and the attempt to usurp divine glory. His empire, imbued with knowledge and might, ultimately exemplifies the potential and the peril of human ambition unrestrained by reverence for Jehovah.

In contemplating the grandeur of the Egyptian pyramids, it is possible to see echoes of Nimrod's legacy— a reflection of humanity's profound capabilities when channeling the remnants of a nearly perfect intellect, albeit in defiance of divine authority. This historical conjecture does not derive from biblical text but rather from reading between the lines of human history, scrutinizing the vestiges of a world both pre- and post-diluvian, forever altered by the ambitions of the first post-flood tyrant.

The Shinar Sidetrack: From Babel's Confusion to Egypt's Construction

The events following the Great Flood, as narrated in the Scriptures, unveil a remarkable progression from the valleys of Shinar to the plains of Egypt, bridging the account of Babel's confusion with the monumental construction of the Egyptian pyramids. To understand this connection deeply, it is essential to trace the linguistic, cultural, and intellectual journey that stemmed from the dispersion at Babel, as it has profound implications for the construction capabilities demonstrated in Egypt shortly thereafter.

The Confusion at Babel: A Linguistic Pivot

The account of Babel, found in Genesis 11:1-9, tells of humanity's united attempt to build a city and a tower "with its top in the heavens." The Hebrew phrase וְרֹאשׁוֹ בַשָּׁמַיִם (*verosho ba-shamayim*) implies an ambition to make a name for themselves, indicative of pride and potential idolatry. Jehovah, observing their actions, intervenes by confounding their language, causing them to scatter across the earth. The term בָּלַל (*balal*) denotes a mixing or confounding, illustrating a sudden shift in the communicative fabric of society. This divine action not only creates immediate disarray but sets the stage for a dispersion of knowledge and skills across the globe, including architectural and construction skills that would be vital for future civilizations.

Dispersion to Egypt: Knowledge Transmission

The descendants of Noah, carrying the intellectual heritage of pre-Flood humanity, would have possessed substantial practical knowledge, including architecture, astronomy, and agriculture. These skills would have been preserved through oral traditions and practical application, much like the Hebrew word מָשָׁל (*mashal*) represents both a proverb and a ruling, denoting wisdom transmitted through word and deed. As these dispersed groups settled in regions like Egypt, they brought with them this compounded knowledge.

Egypt's Intellectual Inheritance: Pre-Pyramid Foundations

Egypt, with its fertile lands and strategic location, became a cradle for early postdiluvian civilizations. The descendants of those who came from Babel may have carried the intellectual vestiges of a world before Babel's confusion. Given the longevity of life spans still in the hundreds of years post-Flood, there was ample opportunity for knowledge retention and enhancement, paralleling the Hebrew concept of דּוֹר לְדוֹר (*dor le-dor*), or "generation to generation." Thus, the intellectual foundation for complex construction in Egypt may have had its conceptual origins in the pre-Babel world.

Construction Wisdom: From Tents to Pyramids

Cain's lineage, as mentioned in Genesis 4:17-22, shows the first recorded instance of city-building and advances in tool-making. This indicates an established understanding of complex structures and the use of advanced technology. After the Flood, Noah's descendants would have retained this knowledge. As Genesis 9:20 states, Noah himself was a man of the soil, familiar with cultivation and, by extension, the manipulation of the earth for various purposes, including construction.

Nimrod's Legacy: Post-Flood Prowess

Nimrod, as described in Genesis 10:8-10, was a mighty one on the earth and a mighty hunter in defiance of Jehovah. The phrase גִּבֹּר צַיִד לִפְנֵי יְהֹוָה (*gibbor tsayid lifnei Jehovah*) emphasizes his prowess and rebellious spirit. His kingdom began in Shinar, which became the epicenter of the unified human effort to build Babel. Although this project was halted, it is likely that the advanced construction techniques and organizational skills required for such an undertaking did not simply vanish with the dispersion. These skills would have been diffused among the various family groups as they spread out from Shinar, with some of these groups eventually making their way to Egypt.

The Egyptian Context: A Confluence of Influences

Egypt, a new focal point for these dispersed groups, was fertile ground for the application of their accumulated knowledge. The pyramids, massive stone structures, are a testament to an advanced understanding of geometry, physics, and engineering. The precise alignment of the pyramids with astronomical points suggests a continuity of pre-Flood and post-Babel knowledge of the heavens, an understanding that echoes Job's reference to the "ordinances of the heavens" in Job 38:33.

Intelligence Unleashed: Building Beyond Babel

The intellect of early postdiluvian humans, though diluted from the pre-Flood peak, was still significantly advanced. In an era when life spans were elongated, the accumulation of wisdom over centuries, combined with the human spirit's innate drive to create and build as exemplified in Exodus 35:31-32 with Bezalel's craftsmanship, could have led to construction capabilities that modern scholars are still striving to comprehend fully. The Hebrew term חָכְמַת לֵב (*chokhmat lev*), or "wisdom of heart," embodied by the craftsmen of the tabernacle, can be paralleled with the intellectual and practical wisdom that would have been required to construct the pyramids.

The Enduring Mystery: Construction Secrets Preserved

While the exact methods employed in the pyramid construction remain debated, it is clear that the builders had access to techniques and knowledge that have not been entirely understood or replicated in modern times. This gap in understanding speaks to a loss of specific technical knowledge over time, which may have been possessed by the pyramid builders in light of their proximity to the original source of human intelligence and longevity post-Flood.

Conclusion: Bridging Babel and Egypt

In sum, the story of humanity's journey from the plains of Shinar to the construction sites of Egypt is one of dispersion, adaptation, and the persistence of ancient wisdom. The linguistic pivot at Babel scattered not only peoples but also their collective knowledge, some strands of which were woven into the fabric of Egyptian society and monumental architecture. The echoes of early human intelligence, coupled with divine providence and the indomitable human spirit, resulted in the enigmatic structures that stand to this day as a testament to a time when heaven seemed a little closer to earth, and the minds of men grasped the fringes of a nearly forgotten perfection.

Peleg's Era

Timing the Tower and the Dispersion of Nations

The era of Peleg is a critical juncture in biblical chronology and the unfolding narrative of humanity post-Flood. The Book of Genesis provides a genealogical and event-based framework through which we can trace the dispersal of nations following the confounding of language at Babel. This event coincides with the lifespan of Peleg, a figure often referenced in the context of this global dispersion. In order to understand the implications of this period, we must delve into the interplay of language, longevity, and the diffusion of antediluvian knowledge.

Chronological Context: The Life Span of Peleg

Peleg's time, as recorded in *Genesis 10:25*, is noted for the division of the earth's population—a direct allusion to the Babel incident. Peleg lived 239 years, a significant decrease from the near-millennial lifespans prior to the Deluge. Yet, this era remained one where individuals like Shem could witness developments centuries apart, providing a bridge of knowledge spanning generations.

The Lingual Shift: Babel's Aftermath

The account of Babel in *Genesis 11* reveals a divine intervention that forever altered human communication. The Hebrew root בלל *(balal)* signifies a mixing or confounding, a vivid depiction of the sudden linguistic fragmentation. Jehovah's intervention was not a gradual linguistic evolution but an instantaneous multiplicity of tongues. Each family unit found themselves linguistically isolated, compelling them to band together with those of shared speech. It was an act that ensured humanity's compliance with the divine mandate to fill the earth (*Genesis 9:1*).

The Intellectual Echoes of Antediluvian Wisdom

The dispersion from Babel carried forth a diminished yet still potent form of antediluvian intelligence. The initial descendants of Adam bore a mental acuity that was considerably closer to the original perfection. Even as lifespans waned, the vestiges of this primeval intellect were preserved, in part, through the longevity of post-Flood figures and the oral traditions they sustained.

Engineering Acumen: Building Beyond Babel

The post-Babel generations wielded the skills and knowledge of their predecessors, seen in the architecture and civilization-building endeavors that followed. Nimrod, a descendant of Ham, exemplifies this as he establishes the first kingdom in the land of Shinar and becomes known for his might—a prowess possibly reflecting more than physical strength but also a commanding understanding of organization and construction.

Tracing Technological Lineage

The story of Cain's lineage points to a proliferation of skills among humanity. While the pre-Flood civilization perished, their technological and constructional abilities did not. It is reasonable to infer that Noah and his sons, being of that antediluvian world, would carry forward the architectural knowledge of their forebears. This continuity of skill is crucial in considering the feats achieved by the dispersed nations, such as the Egyptians.

The Mystery of the Pyramids: A Legacy of Antediluvian Ingenuity

As we ponder the pyramids of Egypt, constructed within the lifetime of Abraham, we must account for the intellectual heritage possibly inherited from the tower builders of Babel. Could the grandeur of these monuments be the tangible manifestation of a once near-perfect intellect, now shrouded in time? It seems plausible that the pyramid builders were beneficiaries of an ancient knowledge that modernity can barely grasp.

The Dispersion's Demographic Implications

The demographic shifts post-Babel had far-reaching implications. Families, now nations, ventured forth carrying fragments of a once-unified human knowledge. They adapted to new lands, developing diverse cultures. Yet, despite the diversification, certain core capabilities—such as construction, agriculture, and metallurgy—were retained, enabling them to establish sophisticated societies like that of Egypt.

Reconciling Biblical Chronology with Egyptian Monumentality

Biblical chronology places the construction of the Egyptian pyramids within a historical context where lifespans were still measured in centuries. This perspective allows for the possibility that individuals contributing to the pyramids' construction could have retained an extraordinary cognitive capacity and technical expertise. Such intellectual fortitude, combined with a longer temporal canvas upon which to refine their knowledge, might elucidate the pyramids' enduring enigma.

Peleg's Epoch: A Time of Transition and Triumph

The era of Peleg stands as a testament to a world in transition—from the aftermath of the Flood to the establishment of nations each bearing the imprints of an intellectual prowess that was in slow decline. It was a time when the shadows of a nearly forgotten perfection still loomed large over human endeavors, echoing through the annals of history in the form of monolithic structures that defy time.

The dispersion during Peleg's time is not merely a historical footnote but a pivotal chapter in humanity's story. It is a period marked by both the loss and preservation of knowledge—a dichotomy best captured in the enigmatic grandeur of the Egyptian pyramids. These structures stand as a testament to human capability, a capability that, though diminished from its antediluvian zenith, was formidable enough to leave a mark that millennia have not erased.

From Babel to Giza: The Journey of Skills and Sagacity

The story of human progress from the immediate post-Flood era to the construction of the Egyptian pyramids is a narrative steeped in the interweaving of divine intervention, human ingenuity, and the relentless pursuit of posterity through architectural marvels. To excavate the depths of this history, one must examine the scriptures, the linguistic shifts, and the transference of skills within the framework of a diminished, yet still potent, human sagacity inherited from an age closer to creation.

The Linguistic Legacy of Babel

The event at Babel (*Genesis 11*) did more than disperse humanity across the face of the earth; it birthed the multiplicity of languages that continue to characterize human societies. The term בלל *(balal)* encapsulates the mixing or confounding that occurred, marking a divine interjection into human history that would force the migration of families and, with them, the spread of knowledge. Each language group, carrying a distinct set of skills and an intellectual heritage that was but a few generations removed from the antediluvian patriarchs, ventured forth to establish new civilizations, each with its unique expressions of their shared legacies.

Nimrod's Empire and the Art of Building

Nimrod, a mighty one on the earth (*Genesis 10:8-9*), exemplifies the post-Babel human condition—a potent combination of the residual intellect from a nearly perfect creation and the drive to make a name in defiance of divine mandate. The term "mighty" (גִּבּוֹר *gibbor*) implies strength, which in Nimrod's context may extend beyond the physical to encompass an intellectual and organizational prowess. His kingdom, beginning in the land of Shinar, became the cradle of urbanization and architectural innovation post-Flood, setting precedents for future builders, including those in Egypt.

The Perseverance of Antediluvian Ingenuity

The descendants of Adam, particularly those before the Flood, possessed an intellectual capacity almost touching perfection. With long lives came the ability to amass extensive knowledge, especially in the art of construction, as seen in the cities built by Cain (*Genesis 4:17*). Though the Flood had swept away that civilization, it did not eradicate the knowledge possessed by Noah and his family. Shem, living contemporaneously with Abraham, served as a human conduit for this precious knowledge, which would have been pivotal in the construction of early postdiluvian structures and eventually, the pyramids.

The Confounding at Babel and the Spread of Knowledge

The dispersion at Babel represented a forced but strategic diffusion of this knowledge across the globe. As families settled in new lands, the initial unity of human thought and language gave way to diversity in expression but unity in skill. The שֵׂכֶל *(sekel)* or wisdom required for building did not diminish as quickly as language diversified; thus, the builders of the pyramids likely capitalized on a rich heritage of construction knowledge. The pyramids' precise engineering and astronomical alignment are a testament to this inherited sagacity.

The Pyramids: Echoes of Edenic Brilliance

The pyramids, arising from the desert sands of Giza, stand as monuments to human capability and the enduring legacy of a knowledge that traces back to Eden. It's plausible that the pyramid builders were the intellectual progeny of Babel's builders, retaining a semblance of the pristine wisdom granted at creation. Their construction demonstrates not just an understanding of geometry and engineering but also an administrative capacity to organize labor and resources on a grand scale—a feat that aligns with the depiction of Nimrod as a powerful leader and builder.

The Biblical and Egyptian Chronological Correlation

Scriptural chronology and Egyptian history intersect at a point where human lifespans, though diminished from their antediluvian peaks, remained significantly longer than today. This allowed for an overlap of generations, wherein the experiences and knowledge of centuries could be shared and retained. Abraham's life overlapped with those who could have been direct or indirect contributors to the pyramids, suggesting that he lived in an era where the knowledge required to build such structures was accessible.

Sagacity and Stone: The Culmination of a Divine Image

Human beings, created in the divine image (*Genesis 1:27*), possessed an inherent capacity for creativity and understanding, which was most vividly displayed in their ability to manipulate the earth's resources to their benefit. The Egyptian pyramids, therefore, may be viewed as the culmination of this God-given potential, expressed within the bounds of a world that had dramatically changed post-Flood.

The Shadow of Antediluvian Longevity: An Era's Impact on Egypt

The impact of Shem's era—marked by extraordinary longevity and closeness to human perfection—on the construction of the Egyptian pyramids is profound yet indirect. While Shem himself resided in Ur and did not have a physical presence in Egypt, the period in which he lived overlapped with the early dynastic periods of Egyptian history. This era was characterized by individuals who still experienced the vestiges of pre-Flood longevity and intellectual prowess.

Echoes of a Lost Perfection

During Abraham's time, people like Shem, who was of a generation much closer to the perfection of Eden, were still alive. Their long lifespans allowed for a continuity of skills and knowledge that could span several centuries. As such, the architectural and organizational feats achieved in Egypt can be seen as resonating with the echo of a world where humans lived for hundreds of years and accumulated vast reservoirs of knowledge and wisdom.

The Transgenerational Transmission of Knowledge

The remarkable longevity of individuals in the generations following the Flood facilitated a transgenerational transmission of knowledge and experience. Even though Shem did not step foot in Egypt, the extended lifespans of such patriarchs meant that the knowledge of antediluvian architecture, astronomy, and administration did not vanish with the deluge but was preserved and disseminated across the generations. This allowed for a robust preservation and sharing of intellectual heritage that would have been indispensable to societies building structures as complex as the pyramids.

The Indirect Influence of a Distant Sage

As a contemporary to some of the patriarchs who may have witnessed or learned about the pyramids' construction, Shem represents a living link to the antediluvian age. The pyramid builders, while not directly instructed by Shem, would have been part of a world that was still feeling the ripple effects of the pre-Flood era's intellectual achievements. The long lifespans allowed for an enduring oral tradition and the retention of a level of expertise that would have been critical in advancing monumental architecture.

Inherited Wisdom in Stone

Thus, while Shem's wisdom was nurtured in Ur, it is conceivable that the intellectual legacy he embodied could have indirectly found its way to the Nile through the network of trade, migration, and the commonality of post-Flood human experience. The construction of the pyramids, therefore, may not reflect a single line of transmitted knowledge from Shem but rather the broader diffusion of antediluvian wisdom that pervaded the post-Flood world.

The shadow cast over Egypt by the era of Shem and his contemporaries is not one of direct influence but rather an overarching presence of a bygone age of heightened human capability. The pyramids stand as a testament not to the presence of a particular individual from that era in their midst but to the enduring legacy of a time when the human condition bore a closer resemblance to its original, divinely intended state of perfection. It is within this broader context that we can appreciate the construction of the pyramids as a historical milestone in humanity's ongoing journey of discovery and achievement.

Pyramid Builders' Paradox

How Ancient Wisdom Trumps Modern Understanding

In a world where modern technology marvels at its own accomplishments, the enigma of the Egyptian pyramids stands as a humbling reminder of ancient wisdom. This structure, born from the minds of men whose lifespans defy modern comprehension, presents a paradox. Their creations eclipse our understanding, hinting at a cognitive depth nurtured by an almost-mythic longevity and purity of thought that, from a Biblical perspective, is irrevocably linked to the proximity of humanity's creation.

The Longevity Lever of Wisdom

The patriarchs of old, figures like Shem (שֵׁם), lived in an epoch when the echoes of Eden's intellectual brilliance still resonated within the human mind. Lifespans stretching hundreds of years were not merely chronological markers but conduits for the accumulation and refinement of knowledge. These were minds that had the capacity to observe, over centuries, the celestial bodies' dance and decipher the principles of geometry, physics, and architecture needed to erect such edifices as the Giza pyramids.

Shem's Chronological Context and its Implications

Consider Shem, who saw the pre-Flood world and lived 150 years into Abraham's lifetime. This was a man whose life, in the UASV translation of the Bible, is described in terms that reflect a bridge between worlds—worlds of the earliest human ingenuity and the one post-Flood where the art of building would come to create wonders like the pyramids. The wisdom available to such a figure, even if not directly imparted to the Egyptians, was part of a broader milieu of knowledge. His era witnessed the Tower of Babel, where the dispersal of humanity carried with it threads of antediluvian understanding, perhaps threads that wove into the fabric of Egyptian society and its monumental achievements.

Cognitive Continuity and Constructive Capacity

The human mind, as reflected in Genesis (בְּרֵאשִׁית), was initially designed for perfection, a perfection that would have engendered an unparalleled cognitive capacity. The antediluvian patriarchs, while not reaching the millennia-long lifespans of Adam or Methuselah, nevertheless possessed lifespans that allowed them to become repositories of wisdom and expertise. This was a time when the mastery of complex tasks and the understanding of the natural world would have been compounded over long lives. The longevity of these early humans meant that their mental faculties were sustained over time spans that allowed for the gestation and perfection of ideas. It is reasonable to surmise that the pyramids' builders benefited from this cumulative wisdom passed down through generations.

The Lingering Light of Antediluvian Intellect

One could argue that the dispersal at Babel (בָּבֶל), resulting in the formation of various language groups, did not completely sever the lines of communication between those ancient wisdom-keepers and the nascent societies that emerged thereafter. While languages fragmented, the essential knowledge for survival and progress—knowledge potentially encompassing advanced mathematics, astronomy, and engineering—would have been a common need among all peoples, including those who settled in Egypt.

The Dilemma of the Dispersed Disciplines

As the descendants of Noah's family moved away from Babel, they carried with them the seeds of civilization. Families would preserve snippets of pre-Babel intellect through oral traditions, stories that encapsulated not just myths but methodologies. This diffusion of knowledge may not have been uniform, but the construction of the pyramids suggests that the Egyptians, whether through a direct or circuitous path, inherited a significant measure of this ancient wisdom.

The Engineering Enigma of Egypt

The pyramids' precision and astronomical alignment hint at an understanding of mathematics and cosmology that bewilders the modern mind. Such knowledge is not easily acquired but rather developed over extensive periods, suggesting a link to an age where human faculties were sharper and lifespans longer. If a mind like Einstein's, in the span of 76 years, could unravel the secrets of relativity, how much more could be achieved by those whose intellectual horizon spanned centuries?

The Lost Legacy of Longevity

What modern scholars often attribute to alien intervention or lost civilizations may well be the fruit of what the Bible suggests about early human potential. This perspective does not devalue the remarkable achievements of ancient Egyptians but places them within a continuum of human history that is biblically consistent. It sees the pyramids not as anomalies but as apexes of human capability, a capability that has dimmed as lifespans shortened and humanity grew further from its original state.

The Conundrum of Chronology and Capability

The Biblical chronology sets a framework for understanding the pyramids' construction within the context of human history. If we take seriously the genealogies and lifespans presented in the Scriptures, then the wisdom required to build such structures was not alien or anachronistic but rather the vestige of an age where human potential was only beginning to wane from its Edenic zenith.

Conclusion: The Paradox as a Portal to the Past

In conclusion, the paradox of the pyramids serves as a portal through which we glimpse the vestiges of a lost pre-Flood world—a world where the human mind bore closer resemblance to its Creator's intent. This perspective challenges the modern narrative, suggesting that what we view as ancient and archaic may indeed hold secrets surpassing our contemporary understanding. Thus, the pyramids stand not solely as tombs or temples but as testaments to a time when ancient wisdom, preserved through longevity and distilled through generations, laid stones that still defy the sands of time.

Echoes of Eden: The Genius of the Early Post-Flood Generations

The narrative of human history is punctuated by moments of profound ingenuity, none perhaps as mystifying and awe-inspiring as the construction of the Egyptian pyramids. The clues to this ancient intelligence are scattered throughout the biblical narrative, particularly in the early post-Flood generations, whose lifespans and proximities to perfection provided fertile ground for unprecedented cognitive feats.

From Eden to Egypt: A Legacy of Learning

In the wake of the Deluge, humanity was presented with a vastly altered world. The patriarchs, with lifespans that dramatically exceed our current three-score and ten, were the bearers of a legacy that began in Eden—a legacy of near-perfect intellect. The book of Genesis (בְּרֵאשִׁית) details the lives of these postdiluvian figures, such as Shem, who witnessed the antediluvian world and carried its wisdom over into a new era, marked by significant changes in human longevity and conditions on Earth.

This intellectual heritage, steeped in centuries of observational learning and oral tradition, was not solely a compendium of facts or tales but a reservoir of deep understanding about the world. The lives of these individuals, such as Methuselah, who walked the earth for 969 years, provided a continuity of knowledge, bridging the antediluvian and postdiluvian worlds.

Decoding the Lifespan: Longevity as a Catalyst for Knowledge

The lifespans recorded in the Scriptures are not merely chronological markers; they signify the potential for a depth of understanding that far exceeds modern capabilities. Shem, living 600 years, and his contemporaries would have amassed a breadth and depth of knowledge almost unimaginable today. It is plausible to conceive that in these lengthy lives, skills and crafts, such as those required for pyramid construction, were refined to a level of sophistication that modernity struggles to comprehend.

These extended years would have provided ample time for the refinement of various disciplines, including architecture and engineering. The biblical figure of Jabal, as noted in Genesis 4:20, was the progenitor of those who dwell in tents and raise livestock, indicating a diversification of skills early in human history. Lamech's descendant Tubal-cain, a forger of tools of copper and iron, exemplifies the early mastery of metallurgy (Genesis 4:22). It is this caliber of skill and knowledge, honed over centuries, that may have been applied to the engineering marvels of the ancient world.

Nimrod and the Tower of Babel: Rebellion and the Diffusion of Knowledge

Nimrod, described as a mighty hunter *before* Jehovah (Genesis 10:9), presents an intriguing figure in post-Flood civilization. His establishment of cities and towers is a testament to the advanced organizational and construction skills present at the time. The Tower of Babel serves as a historical fulcrum, a point at which the unity of human language and purpose was confounded. Yet, the dispersion of people following the confusion of languages did not lead to a loss of knowledge; instead, it facilitated the spread of these early post-Flood civilizations' intellectual and technical prowess across the globe.

As families and languages diverged, they carried with them the seeds of Eden's wisdom, now adapted and applied to new environments. The transition from a universal language to a diversity of tongues may have hindered some collaborative efforts, but it did not erase the collective memory of antediluvian techniques and understandings.

The Egyptian Enigma: A Convergence of Divine Knowledge and Human Ingenuity

Egypt's pyramids stand as a testament to the remarkable capabilities of early post-Flood generations. Their construction required a blend of astronomy, mathematics, and physical engineering—disciplines that, according to biblical chronology, would have been within the reach of those whose intellect was only a few steps removed from the brilliance of Eden. The descendants of

Noah, living several hundred years, would have had the time to refine these disciplines and integrate them into the fabric of their societies.

One must consider the context in which the pyramids were built. Abraham, who lived to see 175 years, was a contemporary to the pyramid age. It is within this overlap of the Abrahamic era and the pyramid builders that we glimpse the potential for an exchange of knowledge and expertise.

Synthesis of Scripture and Stone: A Biblical Interpretation of the Pyramids

To contemplate the intelligence of these generations, one must consider the cumulative effect of nearly unblemished genetics, centuries of life experience, and a proximity to creation's perfection. The pyramids might not only represent a zenith of ancient architecture but also a collective pinnacle of post-Flood human intellect.

The Bible provides us with a framework for understanding this phenomenon. For instance, the lifespan of Shem, which extended into Abraham's era, suggests that there was a continuity of knowledge from the pre-Flood world. In the centuries following the Flood, this knowledge would have been critical in re-establishing civilization and accomplishing feats such as the building of the pyramids.

In examining the Hebrew Scriptures, we find that the term *chokmah* (חכמה), often translated as "wisdom," embodies a comprehensive understanding that includes skill, craftsmanship, and the practical application of knowledge. Proverbs 8:1 portrays wisdom as calling out, personifying it as an active, accessible force in the world. This *chokmah* was not lost with the confounding of language at Babel; instead, it seems to have been embedded in the very fabric of human endeavor, finding expression in structures such as the pyramids.

Conclusion: The Legacy of Antediluvian Intellect in the Post-Flood World

The echo of Eden's intellectual legacy resonates through the annals of post-Flood history, encapsulated in the monumental achievements of early human civilizations. The Egyptian pyramids stand as a testament not merely to the architectural acumen of the ancients but also to the enduring genius bestowed upon humanity in the nascent moments of creation. Through the lens of Scripture, we can discern that the brilliance required to conceive and construct such edifices is a direct lineage of the divine image, a vestige of Edenic wisdom, that once permeated the human soul.

In this, the pyramids are not an anomaly but an affirmation of the extraordinary potential imbued within humanity from its inception—an echo of the divine *dunamis* (δύναμις) that resonated through the antediluvian world and continued to manifest in the centuries that followed the Flood, a testament to the genius of the early post-Flood generations.

Ancient Wits, Modern Mysteries

Why Today's Tech Can't Top Pyramid Ingenuity

The ingenuity that conceived the Egyptian pyramids remains an enigmatic hallmark of ancient intelligence, a marvel that modern technology struggles to parallel. The construction of these monumental edifices at a time when humanity was emerging from antediluvian origins prompts a profound reflection on the cognitive capabilities of early post-Flood humans. It beckons the question: What was it about their intellect that enabled such architectural feats, which seem to defy replication even with today's advanced technology?

The Antediluvian Mind: A Portrait of Pre-Flood Intelligence

The Bible elucidates the remarkable longevity of pre-Flood humans, with lifespans nearing a millennium (Genesis 5). With such extended lives, the accumulation of knowledge and the sharpening of intellect were almost a given. Think of a mind, closer to perfection due to its proximity to the original creation, acquiring wisdom for hundreds of years. These minds, as depicted in Genesis 2:7, were not just carriers of a soul; they *were* living souls, embodying both physical and intellectual vitality.

The Hebrew term *tevunah* (תְּבוּנָה) conveys the idea of insight or understanding. When applied to individuals like Noah and his immediate descendants, we catch a glimpse of an intellectual acuity capable of comprehending not only the present but the mechanics of creation itself. Such *tevunah* would have been essential in designing an ark (Genesis 6:14-16) or, later, monumental structures like the pyramids.

Post-Deluge Dynamics: Shem to Babel and Beyond

Following the Flood, while the lifespan of humans decreased rapidly, the legacy of antediluvian *chokmah* (חכמה), or wisdom, persisted. Shem, Noah's son, lived for centuries, his life overlapping with Abraham, known as the friend of Jehovah (Isaiah 41:8). The longevity of these men, although shorter than their antediluvian ancestors, still permitted a considerable transfer of knowledge and wisdom, potentially contributing to the architectural advancements witnessed in structures such as the pyramids.

Nimrod: The Ambitious Monarch and His Impact

Nimrod, a figure of might and ambition post-Flood, exemplifies the prowess of early humans in consolidating power and directing large-scale projects (Genesis 10:8-10). His drive, though portrayed negatively in the Scriptures due to his defiance (*liph·neh'*) of Jehovah, also suggests a capacity for organization and administration that could be channeled into colossal construction endeavors, akin to the pyramids.

Technological Legacy: From Eden to Egypt

The Bible intimates that pre-Flood humanity had developed a level of technology sufficient to forge tools of copper and iron (Genesis 4:22). This technological acumen, transmitted across the Deluge, would have been instrumental in the pyramid construction process. Consider the *chokmah* required to quarry, transport, and precisely place stones weighing several tons. It's a task that today's machinery accomplishes with brute force but which the ancients achieved with a blend of skill, knowledge, and possibly lost techniques.

The Confusion at Babel: Dispersing Knowledge

At Babel, Jehovah disrupted a unified language, resulting in a scattering of people groups (Genesis 11:7-9). This dispersion meant that the collective *tevunah* was now fragmented, distributed among various language families. Yet, this did not impede the architectural achievements to follow, as each group would have carried with them a portion of the antediluvian intellect and wisdom. The construction of the pyramids might be viewed as a manifestation of this preserved knowledge.

The Imprint of Perfection on Imperfect Minds

If the near-perfection of early humans lent them an edge in terms of intellectual capacity, then their descendants, although further removed from that perfection, still bore the imprint of that original excellence. This is not to say that individuals like Albert Einstein, with a much-shortened lifespan and further from perfection, were not geniuses in their own right. But those who were closer in time to the perfection of Eden had minds less encumbered by the cumulative effects of sin and imperfection, potentially enabling them to understand and manipulate their world in ways that remain mysterious to us.

Innovative Suppositions: From Scripture to Stone

The pyramids stand as silent witnesses to the cognitive greatness that once was. They provoke the postulation that the ancients possessed a *dunamis* (δύναμις), a power or ability that has been diluted over generations. Modern scholars and archaeologists can only speculate on the precise methods used, pointing to the potential of lost techniques and forgotten wisdom.

The Dichotomy of Durability: Temporal Bodies, Timeless Achievements

While our physical bodies have become more susceptible to decay post-Flood, as seen in the decreasing lifespans after Noah, our ability to create structures that withstand the test of time has not necessarily diminished. The pyramids are a testament to the enduring legacy of human *chokmah*, a challenge to the modern mind to rediscover and perhaps, reimagine the capabilities of those who came before us.

In conclusion, the construction of the Egyptian pyramids by minds perhaps not yet fully dulled by the millennia of human imperfection is a mystery that compels us to look backward with admiration and forward with aspiration. Their creation stands as a testament to the remarkable intellectual endowment of early post-Flood humanity, an endowment that raises as many questions as it answers about the capabilities of ancient peoples and the untapped potential of the human mind.

Echoes of Antediluvian Ingenuity: Drawing Parallels Between Biblical Narratives and the Pyramids

In the study of ancient structures like the Egyptian pyramids, we encounter echoes of antediluvian (pre-Flood) ingenuity that seem to parallel the narratives found in the Hebrew Scriptures. To fully grasp the profundity of such structures, one must delve into the Biblical context and historical backdrop from which this ancient wisdom might have emerged.

Pre-Flood Intelligence and Longevity The narrative in Genesis reveals a world before the Flood where human longevity reached nearly a millennium (Genesis 5). The antediluvian patriarchs had lifespans that afforded them centuries of knowledge accumulation and experience. Adam's direct descendants would have had immense *chokmah* (wisdom) and *binah* (understanding), given their closeness to the original perfection. These individuals would not only have accumulated practical skills but likely advanced theoretical knowledge that could translate into architectural marvels comparable to, or even surpassing, the pyramids.

Post-Flood Continuity of Knowledge Post-Flood, while lifespans decreased dramatically, the transmission of knowledge for several centuries would have still been possible through overlapping generations. Shem, Noah's son, lived for 150 years into Abraham's lifetime, suggesting a continuity of antediluvian knowledge that could be passed down. The implication is that the earliest post-Flood generations, like Nimrod and those at Babel, would have retained a significant portion of this knowledge.

The Case of Nimrod and Babel Nimrod, described as a mighty hunter *liphneh* (in opposition to) Jehovah (Genesis 10:9), signifies a character of considerable prowess and capability, potentially also in areas such as construction and organization. The building of the Tower of Babel (Genesis 11) demonstrates not only the ambition of these post-Flood communities but also their significant intellectual and technical abilities. It stands to reason that these abilities could extend to the construction of structures like the pyramids.

Linguistic Dispersion and Technological Dissemination The dispersion at Babel did more than scatter the population; it diversified the pool of knowledge. Each group, carrying with it a unique language and a fragment of the collective expertise, set out to different parts of the world. The migration to places like Egypt would have brought this advanced knowledge, potentially contributing to the construction of the pyramids.

Technological Mastery in a Decreasing Lifespan Even as the post-Flood human lifespan diminished, the early descendants still lived for several centuries, like Abraham. Their longevity, coupled with the *de facto* proximity to a near-perfect human condition, would suggest that their intellectual capacity, though diminished from the antediluvian peak, was still formidable. The knowledge on material properties, engineering, astronomy, and mathematics that would be required to build the pyramids was likely within their grasp.

The Pyramids as a Testament to Lost Wisdom When considering the complexity of the pyramids, it's not merely their scale but their precision that baffles modern science. The alignment with celestial bodies, the mathematical proportions, and the precise cutting and placement of stones suggest a level of knowledge and sophistication that even today is not fully understood. Could this be the vestigial wisdom of a world before the Flood, retained and implemented by post-Flood generations?

Drawing Parallels with Biblical Construction Looking at Biblical construction, from the cities built by Cain's progeny to the Tower of Babel, one sees a progression of construction capability. For example, the use of copper and iron (Genesis 4:22) suggests a mastery over materials that could easily have been applied to the construction of the pyramids. The narrative doesn't just speak of buildings but of cities and towering structures, indicating organized, large-scale projects were within the realm of early human achievement.

Conclusion: A Reflection of the Divine Image in Man Ultimately, the pyramids may serve as a physical reflection of the divine image within man. Even in a state distanced from the perfection of Eden, humans exhibited extraordinary abilities, mirroring the Creator's ingenuity. While the pyramids themselves are not mentioned in the Biblical text, the principles of knowledge, understanding, and skill permeate the narrative from Creation to Babel, providing a plausible context for the kind of achievements represented by the pyramids.

The craftsmanship of the pyramids, therefore, might not only point to the apex of ancient Egyptian civilization but also to a residual brilliance from a humanity once closer to its original, untarnished state—a brilliance that, while dimmed, still yearned to express itself through monumental works that to this day stand as testaments to a forgotten age of human potential.

Frank Conclusions

The hypothesis that antediluvian or immediate post-Flood generations possessed advanced knowledge and capabilities that may have contributed to the construction of such architectural feats does engage with the idea of a transmission of knowledge and the impact of human longevity on ancient civilizations. This idea resonates with those who hold to a literal interpretation of biblical chronology and human history as depicted in the Scriptures.

However, it's important to note that this is a hypothesis that goes beyond the available archaeological and historical evidence concerning the construction of the Egyptian pyramids. The mainstream academic position is that the pyramids were built by the ancient Egyptians using techniques that reflected their own cultural and technological context. The biblical account does not specifically mention the pyramids, nor does it detail the construction methods that might have been used for such projects.

My approach of inferring that post-Flood humans had remarkable intelligence that could have been applied to the construction of the pyramids is an interpretative leap that combines textual analysis with speculative reasoning. While this perspective is not widely accepted within the archaeological community, it represents a unique viewpoint that contributes to the broader conversation about the intersection of faith, scripture, and the interpretation of ancient history.

In the end, whether the extrapolations and inferences drawn are deemed reasonable will largely depend on the worldview and interpretative framework of the individual considering them. For those who share a similar literalist biblical perspective, these ideas may offer a compelling explanation. For others, they may be viewed as an unorthodox approach to the questions surrounding one of the world's greatest ancient mysteries. In the end, isn't this the way it is, a chasm between those who take the Bible literally, using the objective Historical Grammatical Interpretation, and those who use the subjective Historical Critical Method (Higher Criticism)?

CHAPTER 10 The Bible and Science

In The Beginning – Our Planet Earth

The Intersection of Science and Scripture

It's commonly perceived that the realms of modern science and the biblical account of creation are in irreconcilable conflict. Many scientists subscribe to evolutionary theory, proposing that life originated from simple forms millions of years ago. In stark contrast, the Bible presents a picture of distinct creation events, producing organisms that reproduce "according to their kind." Humanity, it states, was sculpted "out of dust from the ground" (Genesis 1:21; 2:7). Yet, is this truly a contradiction, or is there room for deeper understanding?

Charles Darwin's Observations

Charles Darwin, upon his study of finches on the Galápagos Islands, observed variation within a species and theorized a common ancestor for diverse life forms. His concept of natural selection—often summarized as the survival of the fittest—suggested a linear progression from simple to complex organisms. However, what Darwin saw among the finches—variation within a kind—does not disrupt the biblical narrative, which acknowledges the diversity that can arise from a single original type (Genesis 2:7, 22-24).

Does Evidence Support Evolution?

A rigorous examination of the fossil record should reveal transitional forms if evolution from one species to another occurred. Yet, according to some scientists like Francis Hitching, these links are conspicuously absent. This surprising gap could imply support for special creation rather than a gradual evolutionary process. Moreover, living organisms exhibit a high fidelity in replication, resisting changes that would transform them into entirely new species, despite induced mutations.

The Genesis of Life

A longstanding question evolution struggles with is the origin of life. The idea that life could spontaneously arise from non-living matter—once a widely accepted notion—was debunked by the experiments of Louis Pasteur. Today, some propose that life's genesis was due to chance chemical reactions eons ago, under conditions vastly different from today's Earth. Yet, this leap from non-life to life remains a profound mystery, one that aligns more readily with the biblical assertion that life was created by God, aligning with the principle that "life comes from life."

The Stance on Creation

Despite evolution's popularity and its challenges, the belief in creation is often dismissed as unscientific. Yet, such dismissal stems not from empirical evidence but from the presupposition that invoking a Creator falls outside the purview of science. This circular reasoning mirrors that used against miracles. In contrast, the biblical account of creation, particularly in Genesis, offers a coherent narrative for life's complex and unique origins, harmonizing with the concept of an ancient universe and an Earth designed for habitation (Isaiah 45:18).

Scientific Insights and the Bible

The Bible: Not a Science Textbook, Yet Accurate

While the Bible isn't a scientific manual, its statements on natural phenomena are precise. It describes Earth as a sphere "hanging upon nothing" in Job 26:7 and "the circle of the earth" in Isaiah 40:22, imagery that is reminiscent of modern views of our planet in space.

The Earth's Water Cycle and Geological History

The water cycle, crucial for life, is succinctly depicted in Ecclesiastes 1:7, a description that holds true to our current scientific understanding. The dynamic history of mountains, with their rise and fall over eons, is poetically echoed in Psalm 104:6, 8, not contradicting geological findings.

"In the Beginning"

Genesis 1:1 declares the universe's initiation by God, a concept paralleling scientific theories that posit a definite beginning to the cosmos. Though not all scientists endorse the divine aspect, the idea of the universe having a specific inception is widely accepted. Some, like Freeman Dyson, even recognize the possibility of intelligence behind cosmic architecture, suggesting a universe that is not at odds with the idea of a Creator, despite prevailing skepticism.

Conclusion: Coherence Between Science and Scripture

In summation, the perceived chasm between evolutionary theory and the Bible's creation account may not be as wide as some assume. Observations in natural history and the precision of biblical language suggest that there is room for dialogue. The assertion of a universe with a definitive beginning, as stated in Genesis 1:1, is echoed in contemporary scientific understanding, allowing for a perspective that sees the Bible and science as complementary, with the Creator's handiwork evident in the cosmos.

The Orbit of the Earth

When discussing the intersection of the Bible and science, one topic that emerges is the understanding of the Earth's orbit. Some critics assert that the Bible presents an archaic, geocentric view of the universe, whereas others highlight verses that they believe presciently align with modern cosmology.

Biblical Descriptions and Ancient Cosmology

In ancient times, the understanding of the cosmos was radically different from today's heliocentric model. It was believed that the Earth was stationary and that the sun, moon, and stars revolved around it. This view was not unique to the Hebrews but was common across many ancient cultures.

Interpreting Biblical Language

It's essential to recognize that the Bible uses phenomenological language—language of appearance. For instance, when the Psalms speak of the sun's movement, such as in Psalm 19:4-6, the language reflects human observation from the Earth's perspective, not a scientific statement about the structure of the cosmos. Similarly, Ecclesiastes 1:5 which says, "The sun rises, and the sun goes down, and hastens to the place where it rises" uses language that describes the appearance of the sun's movement as seen from the Earth.

Job's Insightful Imagery

However, there are passages within the Bible that hint at a more complex understanding of the cosmos than a simple flat-earth model. For instance, Job 26:7 states that Jehovah "stretches out the north over the void and hangs the earth on nothing." This description is striking, for it aligns more closely with a universe where the Earth is suspended in space, without a visible means of support, which accurately reflects reality.

Isaiah and the Circle of the Earth

In Isaiah 40:22, it is said that Jehovah sits above "the circle of the earth" (*chug* הוג). Some have suggested that this term implies a spherical Earth, although the Hebrew word *chug* could also mean a circular disk. Nevertheless, this scripture does not necessitate a flat-earth interpretation and is not in conflict with a spherical Earth when considering the broad range of meanings.

The Bible and Science – Complementary Not Contradictory

The Bible was not written as a scientific textbook; its purpose was to convey spiritual truths and the moral laws of Jehovah. Thus, when it speaks of natural phenomena, it does so in a way that was understandable to the people of the time without endorsing any particular scientific model. The Bible's primary focus is on God's relationship with humanity, salvation history, and moral instruction.

Reconciling Ancient Texts and Modern Understanding

When reconciling the ancient biblical texts with modern science, it's important to consider the intent and genre of the biblical writings. The poetic books, like Psalms and Job, use metaphorical language to convey truth about God and humanity, not to describe scientific principles. Hence, the Bible and its references to the natural world should be read in light of their literary and historical contexts.

The Cosmological Perspective in Scripture

While the Bible is not a scientific manual, it does not preclude the validity of scientific discovery. Rather, it opens up a framework within which science and faith can coexist. The Hebrew Scriptures provided a foundation upon which a robust understanding of the universe could be built, acknowledging the sovereignty and creative power of

Jehovah without binding believers to a stagnant cosmological model.

In conclusion, when it comes to the Bible and the scientific concept of the Earth's orbit, it is clear that the Bible speaks from the observational viewpoint of its ancient audience. Its descriptions are not intended to be scientific explanations but rather poetic expressions of the wonder and majesty of Jehovah's creation. The passages that seem to touch on aspects of the cosmos do so in ways that are remarkably reflective of a more sophisticated understanding than might be expected from an ancient text, showing that the Bible remains relevant and profound, even as our scientific understanding evolves.

The preciseness of Oxygen and the Complexities of Photosynthesis

In discussing the alignment of the Bible with scientific understanding, the preciseness of oxygen levels on Earth and the process of photosynthesis present intriguing points of consideration. The intricate balance of oxygen necessary for life and the complex biochemical process of photosynthesis is seen by some as pointing to intelligent design, a concept that aligns with the biblical portrayal of Jehovah as the Creator.

Oxygen Balance in Creation

Oxygen is a fundamental element for life as we know it. The current level of oxygen in the Earth's atmosphere is about 21%, a precise figure that sustains life but also limits destructive fires. If the percentage were significantly higher, spontaneous fires could devastate the planet. Conversely, if it were much lower, advanced life forms would struggle to function. Genesis 1:1 states, "In the beginning, God created the heavens and the earth." The balance of oxygen aligns with the assertion that Jehovah created an environment precisely suited for life.

Photosynthesis: A Marvel of Design

Photosynthesis is the process by which green plants and some other organisms use sunlight to synthesize foods from carbon dioxide and water. It involves the green pigment chlorophyll and generates oxygen as a byproduct. In Psalm 104:24, it is said, "O Jehovah, how manifold are your works! In wisdom have you made them all; the earth is full of your creatures." The wisdom of creating a system that recycles carbon dioxide into oxygen — a system essential for life on Earth — is seen as a reflection of divine intelligence.

Interdependence in the Natural World

This process is not just about converting sunlight into energy; it is a foundational component of a much larger system of interdependence that characterizes Earth's ecology. Plants provide oxygen for animals, and in turn, animals provide carbon dioxide for plants — a perfect cycle that speaks to a level of complexity and precision in the natural order. This interdependence can be seen as a physical manifestation of the harmonious design the Bible attributes to Jehovah's creative works.

The Complexity of Chlorophyll

Chlorophyll itself is a complex molecule. Its structure enables it to absorb light most efficiently and transfer it into the energy needed for the synthesis of organic compounds.

The book of Job (Job 38:4-7) echoes the theme of complexity in creation when Jehovah questions Job about the foundations of the earth. The intricate design of chlorophyll and the processes it facilitates could be seen as part of the "measurements" and "foundations" of life that Jehovah laid out.

Scriptural Insights on Natural Laws

While the Bible does not describe photosynthesis or the oxygen cycle in scientific terms, it does acknowledge the natural laws that Jehovah put in place. For example, Jeremiah 33:25 states, "If I have not established my covenant with day and night and the fixed laws of heaven and earth..." This covenant with day and night can be seen as an allusion to the regularity and reliability of natural cycles, which include the cycle of photosynthesis that operates from sunlight (day) and is a foundation for life on Earth.

The Biblical View of Nature's Harmony

The coherence and stability of these natural processes align with the biblical portrayal of nature's harmony under Jehovah's sovereignty. The Psalmist declares in Psalm 148:5-6, "Let them praise the name of Jehovah, for he commanded and they were created. He established them forever and ever; he gave a decree, and it shall not pass away." The laws governing the natural world, including the process of photosynthesis, can be seen as part of this decree.

Miracles and the Natural Order

In the context of miracles, the natural order itself—with its complexity and precision—might be seen as a continuous miracle, an enduring testament to Jehovah's creative power. The Bible suggests that the physical laws that govern the natural world, such as those enabling photosynthesis and maintaining oxygen levels, are a part of God's wise design. While these processes occur without the need for ongoing supernatural intervention, their initial establishment and precise tuning could be perceived as a form of miraculous act, indicative of a wise and powerful Creator. In this way, even as we acknowledge that the age of biblical miracles of overt divine intervention has passed, we can still see in the consistent and reliable workings of nature a kind of standing miracle, an ongoing witness to the wisdom and power of Jehovah as described in the Scriptures.

From Single Cells to Multicellular Man

The journey from the most rudimentary forms of life to the complexity of multicellular organisms, including humans, presents a fascinating intersection of biblical testimony and scientific discovery. The Bible, while not a scientific textbook, does present an account of creation that lays the groundwork for exploring this progression.

The Biblical Account of Creation

The biblical account of creation in the book of Genesis describes a process that progresses from simplicity to complexity. Genesis 1:20-21 says, "And God said, 'Let the waters swarm with swarms of living creatures, and let birds fly above the earth across the expanse of the heavens.' So God created the great sea creatures and every living creature that moves, with which the waters swarm, according to their kinds, and every winged bird according to its kind." The text here underscores the emergence of life in a sequential fashion, highlighting the creation of various "kinds" of living organisms.

Life's Beginning: The Cell

At the most basic level, life begins with the cell, the smallest unit that can be said to be alive. All organisms, from the simplest bacteria to the most complex human, are composed of cells. The intricacy of even a single cell, with its machinery for replication, metabolism, and energy conversion, is a marvel of biological architecture. Psalm 139:14 declares, "I praise you, for I am fearfully and wonderfully made. Wonderful are your works; my soul knows it very well." This sentiment captures the awe-inspiring complexity inherent in living organisms at even the cellular level.

Complexity in Multicellular Life

As the narrative of Genesis continues, it portrays the development of more complex life forms. The movement from aquatic life to terrestrial life is a major step in complexity. In Genesis 1:24, it is written, "And God said, 'Let the earth bring forth living creatures according to their kinds: livestock and creeping things and beasts of the earth according to their kinds.' And it was so." The transition from single-cell organisms to multicellular ones is a significant leap in biological complexity, which is also suggested by this passage.

The Human Body: A Multicellular Marvel

When the Bible reaches the creation of man, the language emphasizes the uniqueness of human beings.

Genesis 1:27 states, "So God created man in his own image, in the image of God he created him; male and female he created them." The human body consists of approximately 37.2 trillion cells, each intricately working together in a symphony of life. The human organism, as described in the Bible, is seen not merely as a physical entity but as a bearer of the divine image, setting humanity apart in the creation narrative.

Scientific Understanding of Multicellularity

Scientifically, the emergence of multicellular organisms from single-celled ancestors is understood to be a product of evolutionary processes. Cells began to aggregate and specialize, leading to greater efficiency and capabilities. The complexity of these organisms increased over time, giving rise to the diversity of life forms we see today.

Harmony of Scripture and Science

While the Bible does not provide a detailed explanation of the scientific mechanisms behind the development from single cells to multicellular organisms, it does frame the emergence of life within the context of divine action. In this sense, the Bible and science speak to different aspects of the same reality: the former in terms of purpose and design, the latter in terms of process and mechanism.

Miracles and Natural Processes

In the context of our understanding of miracles and their purpose, the development of life from single cells to the complex structure of humans could be viewed through a similar lens. The miraculous, in biblical terms, is about God's intervention and revelation to mankind. While the creation account can be seen as miraculous in its own right, the natural processes that science explores—such as the development of life forms—are the means by which Jehovah's creative power and wisdom are continuously demonstrated.

A Testament to Divine Wisdom

In summary, the progression from single-cell life forms to the complexity of humans is both a scientific journey and a testament to the biblical portrayal of Jehovah's wisdom in creation. Each step in the increasing complexity of life can be seen as a reflection of the biblical principle found in Proverbs 3:19: "Jehovah by wisdom founded the earth; by understanding he established the heavens." The amazing process from the simplest life forms to the intricate human body resonates with this theme of divine wisdom and power, even as we recognize that the miracles described in the Bible serve a different, more immediate purpose in God's relationship with humanity.

Was It Simply by Chance?

The question of whether the universe and life itself are products of chance or the result of divine intervention is one that has been debated for centuries. Within the context of the Bible and its perspective on miracles, we must explore the complexities of creation and the statistical probabilities that challenge the concept of a universe created by chance.

The Statistical Improbability of Life

Considering the universe from a statistical standpoint, the odds of life forming by random chance are astoundingly low. The precise conditions required for life to exist—the right kind of elements, the correct range of temperatures, a stable planetary orbit, and numerous other factors—create a narrow window through which life as we know it could emerge. The anthropic principle suggests that the universe appears to be fine-tuned to support life, leading some to conclude that this tuning indicates a purposeful design rather than random chance.

The Complexity of Biological Systems

Within the biological realm, the complexity of living organisms hints at a sophistication that surpasses mere chance. The intricate machinery of the cell, the coded information within DNA, and the highly complex processes that sustain life point to a level of complexity that, to many, suggests intentionality. The concept of irreducible complexity, though controversial in the scientific community, raises the question of how complex biological systems could have formed incrementally through random mutations and natural selection alone.

Biblical Language of Purpose and Design

The Bible itself speaks not in terms of chance but of intentional design. For instance, in the book of Jeremiah 1:5, Jehovah says, "Before I formed you in the womb I knew you, and before you were born I consecrated you; I appointed you a prophet to the nations." This indicates a belief in divine foreknowledge and purpose, contrary to the idea of random chance.

The Miraculous as a Testament to Intention

The Bible's accounts of miracles serve to emphasize the belief in a God who is actively involved in His creation.

Edward D. Andrews

Miracles by their very nature defy the natural order, which is often perceived as being governed by chance and randomness. When Jesus turned water into wine at Cana (John 2:1-11), for instance, it demonstrated a control over the physical elements that implies a creator with authority over nature.

The Laws of Nature and the Hand of God

It is important to note that the laws of nature, which are often cited as mechanisms of chance, do not necessarily negate the possibility of divine design. The regularity and predictability of these laws may actually reflect the orderly mind of a creator. The apostle Paul, in his letter to the Romans (Romans 1:20), states, "For his invisible attributes, namely, his eternal power and divine nature, have been clearly perceived, ever since the creation of the world, in the things that have been made." Here, Paul suggests that the natural world reveals the character of God.

Probability, Complexity, and Divine Action

Examining the probability of the universe's existence and the complexity of life within it, and comparing these observations with the biblical narrative of purposeful creation, we find two contrasting viewpoints: one of chance and randomness, and the other of divine intention and miracle. While science often operates within the framework of chance and probability, the Bible presents a worldview of purpose and divine action.

The Role of Faith in Interpretation

Ultimately, whether one sees the universe as a product of chance or the handiwork of Jehovah requires a leap of faith. Hebrews 11:3 declares, "By faith we understand that the universe was created by the word of God, so that what is seen was not made out of things that are visible." Faith, then, is the lens through which believers interpret the evidence of the world around them, seeing purpose where others might see chance.

The Question of Chance versus Divine Design

In the pursuit of understanding the Bible's stance on miracles and science, the question "Was it simply by chance?" is pivotal. The Bible itself asserts that the complexities of the universe, the exacting conditions for life, and the intricacies of biological systems point to a divine architect rather than a cosmic roll of the dice. The miracles described within its pages serve to underscore this conviction, providing believers with a foundation for faith in a purposeful and intentional creation orchestrated by the sovereign will of Jehovah.

Evolution and Creation

The conversation between science and the Bible about the origins of life and the universe has often been contentious. Many scientists advocate for **evolution**, which suggests that life began from simple forms and diversified over millions of years. The Bible, however, speaks of life being created by Jehovah, with species reproducing "according to its kind" (Genesis 1:21) and man being formed "out of dust from the ground" (Genesis 2:7). Does this present a **conflict** with established scientific thought?

Edward D. Andrews

Observations and Interpretations

The foundational observations made by **Charles Darwin** regarding finches on the Galápagos Islands are, at a basic level, not in conflict with the Bible. The idea that diverse species can come from a common ancestor is reflected in the biblical account, where humanity is described as descending from an original pair (Genesis 2:7, 22-24). Yet, this adaptation within species is quite different from the grander claim of evolution—that all life stems from a singular ancestral form.

The **fossil record** is a critical testing ground for evolutionary theory. Francis Hitching, among other scientists, points to the absence of intermediary links between major groups, which has led to alternative evolutionary models such as punctuated equilibrium. These gaps and the complex mechanisms that maintain species stability are difficult to reconcile with the idea of natural evolution and seem to resonate more with the notion of special creation.

The Origin of Life

When it comes to the origin of life, evolutionists face a substantial hurdle. The spontaneous generation of life from non-life, once believed possible, was debunked by **Louis Pasteur**. The current scientific theory posits life emerged from chemical processes billions of years ago when conditions on Earth were radically different. However, even under altered conditions, the leap from inanimate matter to living cells is vast. Michael Denton articulates the improbability of life sparking into being by chance. Here, the biblical explanation—that life was created by Jehovah—aligns seamlessly with the principle that life comes only from preexisting life.

Why Not Creation

The dismissal of creation largely stems from its association with supernatural causation, which is often seen as unscientific. Yet, the skepticism toward evolution isn't unwarranted; its methodology is not in line with experimental science. Evolutionary theory deals with historical reconstructions that cannot be verified through experimentation or direct observation. It is filled with conjectures and unanswered questions.

The Genesis account, when understood as describing creative 'days' that span long periods, offers a **plausible narrative** for the origin of life. It addresses unique, unrepeatable events in a way that is consistent with the observed order and complexity of life. Therefore, while evolution remains a prevalent theory, it is not without significant challenges, and creation as depicted in the Bible retains its credibility, particularly when we consider the concept of an old Earth and a universe that has existed for billions of years.

What About the Flood?

The account of the global flood as described in the book of Genesis is one of the most striking examples of Jehovah's intervention in human history. For many, the historicity of the Flood serves as a touchstone for the discussion of the Bible's reliability and its consonance with scientific evidence.

Historical Acceptance of the Flood Narrative

Prominent biblical figures, including Isaiah, Jesus, Paul, and Peter, acknowledged the Flood as an actual historical event. These references are not mere allegories but are presented as factual recollections of human history. For instance, Isaiah references the waters of Noah as a standard of Jehovah's promise (Isaiah 54:9). Jesus likened the days of his coming to the days of Noah, implying a literal understanding of the event (Matthew 24:37-39). These acknowledgments in Scripture provide a framework for understanding the Flood as a real occurrence.

The Mechanics of the Flood According to Scripture

Genesis 7:11 describes the onset of the Flood with the phrase "all the fountains of the great deep burst forth, and the windows of the heavens were opened." This vivid description suggests a cataclysmic event involving both subterranean waters and torrential rain from above. The Hebrew term used for "floodgates" (*arubbah*) implies a deluge pouring forth from the heavens, a supernatural unleashing of waters. The "fountains of the great deep" (*ma'yanot tehom rabbah*) could refer to subterranean aquifers or oceanic sources, which, combined with the rain, caused a flood of such magnitude that it covered the mountains.

Scientific Perspectives and the Flood

Modern geology and paleontology often reject the idea of a global flood, citing a lack of worldwide sedimentary evidence and the challenges of housing and feeding all animal species in a single ark. They propose localized flooding or a series of floods to explain the various flood myths that exist in different cultures around the world. These fields tend to favor naturalistic and gradualist explanations over catastrophic events.

Cultural Corroboration of Flood Narratives

Interestingly, flood myths are pervasive in numerous ancient cultures worldwide, with many elements mirroring the Genesis account. These stories could be interpreted as collective memories of a significant historical event, albeit embellished or altered through generations. The widespread nature of these myths suggests that the biblical Flood narrative may have roots in an actual ancient catastrophe remembered by different civilizations.

The Debate over Universality and Extent

The extent of the Flood described in Genesis is a subject of much debate. The text states that the waters prevailed above the mountains (Genesis 7:19-20), suggesting a universal flood. However, some argue for a localized flood, given the practical considerations of gathering all known animal species and the logistics of their survival. The universal perspective, however, sees the Flood as a divine act of judgment and renewal, requiring a miracle beyond natural explanation, consistent with the theme of divine interventions throughout the Bible.

Faith, Interpretation, and the Natural World

Belief in the historicity of the Flood often hinges on faith in the divine inspiration and authority of the Bible. For those who accept the biblical record, the natural world bears the hallmarks of past divine action, possibly including a global deluge. The interpretation of geological and fossil records is seen through this lens, where every layer of sediment and every fossilized remain may hold pieces of the Flood's legacy.

The Flood in Biblical and Scientific Discourse

In the discourse of the Bible and science, the Flood narrative stands as a testament to Jehovah's sovereignty over creation and His moral governance. The account challenges the conventions of modern science with a portrayal of divine power that alters the very fabric of the natural world. While the Flood continues to be a point of contention between biblical literalism and scientific skepticism, it remains a pivotal theme in the exploration of the Bible's miracles and their place in history. Whether seen as myth or history, the Flood narrative invites believers to ponder the power and purposes of Jehovah, as well as the relationship between His Word and the world we observe.

What about the Floodwaters

The Biblical account of the Flood describes an event of such cataclysmic proportions that it reshaped the very topography of the Earth. The question of the Floodwaters—both their source and their recession—is a matter of significant interest when examining the interface between the Bible and science. Let's delve into the scriptural narrative and the scientific considerations relevant to this event.

The Source of the Floodwaters

The account in Genesis describes the deluge as a unique event, where "all the fountains of the great deep burst forth, and the windows of the heavens were opened" (Genesis 7:11). The term "fountains" (מַעְיְנֹת ma'yanot) and "windows" (אֲרֻבֹּת arubbot) signify vast reservoirs of water beneath and above the Earth's surface, as envisioned by the ancient Hebrew cosmology.

Scientific Considerations of Ancient Topography

It is plausible, from a geological perspective, that the pre-Flood topography differed markedly from the present. Lower sea basins and less elevated mountain ranges could suggest a landscape where a universal deluge could be accommodated. Such alterations in the Earth's surface can be attributed to the dynamic nature of plate tectonics. Indeed, the Book of Psalms poetically captures the concept of a dramatically different Earth when it says, "You covered it with the deep as with a garment; the waters stood above the mountains" (Psalm 104:6).

Post-Flood Topographical Reformation

The recession of the Floodwaters, as described in the Biblical text, implies a significant topographical reformation. The waters "receded steadily from the earth" (Genesis 8:3), which might suggest a mechanism similar to what is observed in glacial rebound today. When the immense weight of the floodwaters was lifted, the Earth's crust could have reacted by rising, thus contributing to the current distribution of land and sea.

The Deep Sea Basins and Mountain Ranges

The idea that the current mountains were once plains and the deep sea basins were shallower is consistent with the scientific understanding of the Earth's surface as dynamic and ever-changing. Geological evidence suggests that tectonic activities have caused dramatic changes in the Earth's topography over time.

Continental Plates and Water Recession

The movement of continental plates and the consequent formation of trenches and basins provide a feasible explanation for the drainage of Floodwaters. The narrative of waters "receding" could align with the geological process wherein the sinking of plates at their boundaries allows water to redistribute, effectively draining from the once-flooded landscapes.

Glacial Impact on Earth's Crust

Considering the effects of glacial weight on the Earth's crust, the Flood, a massive and rapid influx of water, could have similarly had a significant impact. The concept is mirrored in today's observation where the removal of glacial ice causes a rebound effect, as noted regarding Greenland's ice.

Convergence of Biblical Narrative and Scientific Possibility

While the historical and scientific inquiry into the Flood continues, the Biblical narrative presents it as a real event, corroborated by subsequent writers and figures within the Scriptures. Isaiah, Jesus, Paul, and Peter affirm its historicity, providing a theological continuity that transcends the mere naturalistic explanation.

In the historical-grammatical interpretation of the Biblical text, the Flood is not a mythical tale but an event with tangible effects on the Earth's topography. The dialogue between the scriptural record and scientific observation allows for a multidisciplinary approach to understanding the great deluge. The changes in the Earth's surface, as reflected in the scriptural account, align with scientific principles, offering a coherent narrative that regards the Floodwaters as a pivotal factor in the Earth's geological history. While the miraculous nature of the event remains within the realm of divine action, its implications resonate through both the ancient text and the scientific landscape.

Health and Sanitation

The exploration of health and sanitation in the context of the Bible and science reveals a remarkable convergence between ancient scriptural mandates and modern public health principles. These ancient prescriptions found primarily in the Mosaic Law reveal a profound understanding of hygiene, diet, and infectious disease control that aligns with contemporary health practices.

Biblical Prescriptions for Cleanliness

The Mosaic Law, as detailed in Leviticus and Deuteronomy, sets forth various laws that pertain to cleanliness. For instance, the Hebrew term *tahor* (טָהוֹר), meaning "clean," and its antonym *tamei* (טָמֵא), meaning "unclean," occur frequently, underscoring a system of health-related behaviors. Washing after handling dead bodies (Numbers 19:11-12) and the isolation of those with infectious diseases (Leviticus 13:4-5) reflect a rudimentary understanding of contamination and the spread of illness.

Dietary Regulations

Dietary laws, such as the prohibition against consuming blood (Leviticus 17:10-14) and certain types of animals deemed unclean (Leviticus 11), can be seen as measures to reduce the risk of zoonotic diseases—the transmission of diseases from animals to humans. The prohibition against pork, for example, considering that pork can be a source of parasites such as trichinella, displays a practical health consideration, even if the original commandment was given in a religious context.

Sanitation Practices

Sanitation practices are explicitly mentioned, such as the commandment for the Israelites to bury their excrement outside of their camp (Deuteronomy 23:12-14). This prescription not only reflects a concern for hygiene but also for the dignity of the individual and the sanctity of the community, where Jehovah's presence was to be acknowledged. Such measures align with modern understanding of waste management to prevent the spread of diseases.

Infectious Disease Control

Quarantine and the concept of isolation of infected individuals have a direct parallel in the Bible. The laws concerning leprosy, often a term used for a variety of skin ailments, required priests to examine and, if necessary, isolate individuals showing symptoms (Leviticus 13). This resembles modern public health protocols for containment of contagious diseases.

Postnatal Care

The purification period following childbirth (Leviticus 12) also bears health considerations. The stipulated time for a woman to remain in a state of *tumah* (impurity) following the birth of a son or daughter provided a period of recovery, recognizing the vulnerability of both mother and child to infection.

Public Health and Community Responsibility

The biblical health laws also indicate a strong community responsibility for health. If a house was found to have signs of mold or decay, it was subject to inspection and possible destruction (Leviticus 14:33-45). This communal aspect of public health underscores the interconnectedness of individual health and community wellbeing.

Scientific Affirmation

What is particularly noteworthy is the extent to which these biblical health laws accord with modern scientific understanding. While the Israelites would not have understood the presence of germs or the detailed mechanisms of disease transmission, the laws given to them helped mitigate the risks of infectious diseases, parasites, and other health threats.

Edward D. Andrews

The Role of Miracles in Health

In the realm of miracles, the Bible does recount instances where Jehovah intervened to address health issues miraculously, such as the healing of Hezekiah's life-threatening illness (2 Kings 20:1-11). These instances, however, do not negate the soundness of the health and sanitation principles provided in the Law, which had everyday applicability and did not rely on miraculous intervention.

The confluence of biblical instruction and scientific validation regarding health and sanitation practices is substantial. It serves to highlight the wisdom embedded within the Scriptures, transcending the purely spiritual realm and venturing into practical, everyday living. These ancient guidelines, predicated on the care and wisdom of Jehovah, anticipated principles that would only be understood and appreciated with the advent of modern science, providing a testament to the depth and enduring relevance of the biblical text.

Are There Scientific Errors in the Bible?

The intersection of the Bible with science often raises questions about the accuracy of the Scriptures in light of modern scientific knowledge. Critics and skeptics have pointed to what they perceive as scientific inaccuracies within the biblical text. Yet, a thorough examination reveals that, although the Bible is not a scientific textbook, when it does touch on matters of scientific nature, it does so accurately and often preempts knowledge that humanity only later discovered through scientific inquiry.

Ancient Understandings and Modern Misconceptions

It is paramount to consider the genre and purpose of the biblical text when evaluating its scientific content. The Bible communicates spiritual truths, moral principles, and historical narratives, not scientific data. Hence, when it refers to natural phenomena, it often does so using phenomenological language—describing things as they appear to the observer without commenting on the physical principles underlying them. For instance, the sun "rises" and "sets" is a common expression, even in modern vernacular, without implying a geocentric cosmology.

Cosmology and the Bible

Critics have often cited biblical passages, like those in Genesis 1, as presenting a cosmology inconsistent with modern astronomy. Yet, the language of Genesis is not prescribing a scientific model but rather employing symbolic and metaphorical language to articulate the creative sovereignty of Jehovah over all realms of the cosmos. The intent is not to offer a scientific treatise but to affirm the divine orchestration of the universe's existence.

The Circle of the Earth

In Isaiah 40:22, it is written that Jehovah sits above "the circle of the earth" (*chug ha-aretz*). The term *chug* does not necessarily denote a flat disc, as some have suggested, but rather can imply roundness or encompassing. The understanding of Earth's shape is nuanced and is not committed to a particular scientific model within this text.

Hydrology and the Bible

The biblical description of the water cycle exhibits remarkable consistency with the modern understanding of hydrology. Ecclesiastes 1:7 describes how "All the rivers run into the sea; yet the sea is not full; unto the place from whence the rivers come, thither they return again." This reflects the cycle of evaporation and precipitation without delving into the scientific details of these processes.

Biology and the Bible

In the field of biology, Leviticus 17:11 states, "For the life of the flesh is in the blood." While the primary context is theological, articulating the rationale for the sacrificial system, it incidentally corresponds with the biological reality that blood is essential for transporting oxygen and nutrients to sustain the body's life.

Medicine and the Bible

The Bible's health laws, some of which were touched upon under the heading of health and sanitation, show a prescient understanding of practices that would prevent the spread of disease—practices not common in other ancient cultures and only validated by modern medicine millennia later.

Astronomy and the Bible

The biblical text also acknowledges the great number of stars in the heavens. Jeremiah 33:22 compares the host of heaven with a number that cannot be counted, an insight that is in harmony with the astronomical fact of the vast, innumerable quantity of stars in the universe.

Geology and the Bible

Job 28:5 speaks of the Earth as having both fire and food—what can be seen as an early reference to the geothermal processes and fertility of the soil. This poetic expression correlates with geological understanding but is expressed within the context of a contemplation on wisdom, rather than a geological dissertation.

The instances in which the Bible refers to natural phenomena do not present themselves as scientific errors when the text is properly understood within its literary and historical context. It is an anachronism to impose a modern scientific standard on an ancient text that communicates in the language of the times and for purposes far beyond the scope of a science textbook. The Bible's occasional anticipatory alignment with scientific principles, whether in cosmology, biology, or other fields, is consistent with the belief in divine inspiration and the timeless relevance of its messages. As the Bible speaks to the human condition across ages, it occasionally intersects with scientific truths not as a primary aim but as a byproduct of its divinely orchestrated communication.

CHAPTER 11 Is Genesis' Creation of the World a Myth and Legend?

The Creation of the World – What Does Genesis Say?

In the annals of history, the opening chapter of the Bible, Genesis, has sparked intense debates and a plethora of interpretations. Critics often dismiss it as mere myth or legend, but such judgments may not do justice to the nuanced narrative that Genesis presents. This pivotal text has been subject to scrutiny, and it is imperative to delve into its content with an objective lens, to unravel whether its account aligns with observable reality, rather than forcing it to conform to preconceived theoretical constructs.

Genesis is not an exhaustive scientific manual; it delineates a sequence of events, spotlighting the "what" and "when" rather than explicating the "how" of creation. The narrative is portrayed through the perspective of an earthly observer, framing celestial bodies like the sun and moon as "luminaries" based on their apparent size and brightness from the vantage point of the ground—not their actual scale in the cosmos. Here, the sun, referred to as a "greater light," and the moon, a "lesser light," serve functional roles for Earth's inhabitants, notwithstanding their true astronomic proportions (Genesis 1:14-18).

The text intimates that the Earth preexisted in a barren state, shrouded in darkness and enveloped by waters, for an indeterminate span before the onset of the first "day"

(Genesis 1:2). The introduction of the Hebrew term *yohm*, typically rendered "day," necessitates a nuanced interpretation. *Yohm* encompasses various durations—from a literal 24-hour period to an epoch or era. As such, the "days" of Genesis are not constrained to modern temporal measurements but could signify lengthy, defined periods of divine activity.

How Long Is a Genesis "Day"?

The duration of a "day" (*yohm*) in the Genesis narrative is a topic of considerable debate. The text itself presents a day as a division of time that encompasses both "evening" and "morning," yet does not explicitly prescribe a 24-hour framework for each creative period. The semantic range of *yohm* allows for substantial flexibility, suggesting that the creative "days" could be epochs extending well beyond the confines of our daily clock cycles (Genesis 1:5; 2:4).

First "Day"

On the inaugural "day," the command "Let light come to be" catalyzed the first act of creation, manifesting light, and demarcating day from night (Genesis 1:3, 5). This emergence of light implies not the creation of the sun but the appearance of sunlight upon the Earth's surface—a pivotal transition from opacity to transparency in the Earth's atmosphere.

Second "Day"

During the second epoch, the creation of an "expanse" (*ra·qi'a'*) separated the waters above from those below (Genesis 1:6-8). This "expanse," often translated as "firmament" or "sky," rejects the mythical conception of a rigid dome. Instead, it denotes the vast stretch of sky that envelopes the Earth—a dynamic and ever-expanding canvas that houses the celestial bodies and the atmosphere.

Third "Day"

The third "day" ushered in the congregation of waters and the revelation of dry land—a remarkable geological transformation indicative of tectonic shifts and continental emergence (Genesis 1:9, 10). This period also saw the genesis of vegetation, seeding the Earth with diverse flora essential for the sustenance of life (Genesis 1:11). The specificity of "kinds" suggests a deliberate design in biodiversity, not an exhaustive inventory of all plant life.

Fourth "Day"

The fourth epoch demarcates the visibility of the sun, moon, and stars in the firmament—celestial markers for timekeeping and signs (Genesis 1:14-16). Here, the text transitions from *'ohr*, general light, to *ma·'ohr'*, specific light-bearers, signifying the discernibility of these sources from the Earth's perspective.

The sequence in Genesis, therefore, articulates a progression of creation that is both methodical and purposeful. It aligns with the concept of a universe governed by order and points to a Creator who designs with intentionality and deliberation. The portrayal of creation in Genesis is far from mythic fantasy; it is a foundational narrative that has shaped centuries of cosmological understanding.

As we peel back the layers of this ancient text, it is crucial to approach it without the tinted lenses of later mythological constructs or modern scientific paradigms. Instead, Genesis invites readers to witness the unfolding of creation as a series of deliberate acts, transcending the bounds of human temporality and encompassing a divine chronology that punctuates the very fabric of time. This respectful examination leads us not into the realm of myth, but into the contemplation of a timeless divine orchestration, echoing through the annals of both history and eternity.

How Did Genesis Know?

The account of creation in the Book of Genesis has, for centuries, stood under the lens of skepticism and incredulity, primarily when placed alongside ancient creation myths. However, an insightful examination of its content, structure, and implications often leads to the compelling question: How did Genesis know? This query arises from the striking alignment of the Genesis account with the order of events as we understand them today, despite its origins in a pre-scientific era.

Genesis in Contrast with Ancient Near Eastern Myths

Unlike the polytheistic and often chaotic creation narratives of ancient Near Eastern cultures, the Hebrew account in Genesis is characterized by a resounding monotheism. The term *bara* (בָּרָא), denoting creation in Genesis 1:1, conveys the sense of bringing into existence something new, something not previously seen, and does so under the singular divine will of Jehovah. This is in stark contrast to the tumultuous cosmogonies of neighboring peoples, which frequently involve a pantheon of gods and deities engaged in conflicts.

Moreover, the Hebrew text uses the word *tohu* (תֹהוּ), "formless," and *bohu* (בֹהוּ), "empty," in Genesis 1:2 to describe the primordial state of the earth. This state of *tohu wabohu* (תֹהוּ וָבֹהוּ), formlessness and emptiness, precedes the divine ordering of the cosmos—a concept absent from the mythologies that are marked by theogonies and cosmic battles.

Scientific Soundness of the Genesis Order

The Genesis narrative delineates creation across ten major stages, from the inception of the cosmos to the creation of man. This sequential order is not merely a didactic tool but also presents a succession that echoes the logical progression of creation as corroborated by various fields of scientific study. It does not delve into specifics that would align it with any modern scientific theory; instead, it presents an ordered progression of creation events that is not contradicted by empirical observations.

The Unlikelihood of Mosaic Guesswork

Considering Moses as the author of Genesis, one might wonder how a man educated in ancient Egypt—a civilization replete with its own set of deities and creation myths—could pen a document with such striking dissimilarities to contemporary mythologies and unintentional alignment with later scientific understandings. The probability that Moses, or any author of the time, could randomly guess the order of creation that aligns with the fossil record and modern cosmology is astonishingly low.

The fossil record, for instance, affirms the sudden appearance of various "kinds" (*miyn*, מִין) of life forms, as stated in Genesis, which produces after their kind (*le-miyn-ehu*, לְמִינֵהוּ), with no transitional forms as required by evolutionary theory (Genesis 1:11-12, 21, 24-25). Each kind of plant and animal appears fully formed, with the potential for variety within the kind, but without the evidence of having evolved from a different kind.

Divine Revelation as the Source of Knowledge

If Moses did not acquire his understanding of the creation order from contemporary sources or through guesswork, one plausible explanation from a Judeo-Christian perspective is divine revelation. The Genesis account may indicate that Moses received insights about creation from Jehovah himself, who, being the Creator, would possess complete knowledge of the sequence and nature of creation events. This perspective positions the Genesis creation narrative not as a myth derived from human imagination but as a record of divine communication.

Linguistic and Structural Analysis

A closer look at the linguistic and structural composition of Genesis further distinguishes it from myth. The use of structured repetition, thematic development, and genealogical records throughout Genesis presents a historical narrative framework rather than mythological storytelling. Phrases such as "And there was evening, and there was morning" (וַיְהִי־עֶרֶב וַיְהִי־בֹקֶר) denote the conclusion of each creative period, underlining a systematic approach to the passage of time and events.

The structured genealogies that begin with Adam in Genesis 5:1 (זֶה סֵפֶר תּוֹלְדֹת אָדָם) and trace the lineage through Noah to Abraham, are presented with meticulous detail. This attention to lineage and historical continuity is typically absent from mythological texts, which often focus on the exploits of gods rather than the precise genealogical records of humanity.

The narrative of Genesis, upon rigorous examination, unfolds not as a myth interwoven with the legends of ancient civilizations but as a unique document that presents a monotheistic and ordered account of creation. Its alignment with known scientific sequences, distinct from and often preceding scientific discovery, alongside its monotheistic purity and detailed genealogies, points to a profound source of knowledge. For those who hold to the veracity of the Hebrew Scriptures, the answer to "How did Genesis know?" is found in the belief that Jehovah, the Creator, imparted this knowledge to the author—a testament to the divine rather than the human origin of this ancient text.

Ancient Creation Stories

In exploring the myriad of ancient creation stories, we find a global phenomenon of rich and varied narratives that attempt to explain the origin of the world. These stories often share common themes, such as the emergence of the world from a primordial state of chaos, the role of gods and divine beings in the creation process, and a cosmic order coming out of disorder. However, they also reflect significant differences and cultural influences, which, from a conservative biblical viewpoint, are seen as distortions of an original truth revealed early in human history.

The Hebrew account of creation in Genesis stands apart from these stories. This uniqueness suggests that, rather than being one myth among many, it preserves a historical account that predates the confusion of languages at the Tower of Babel as described in Genesis 11. The dispersion of people groups across the globe, with their foundational knowledge of creation now fragmented, would have evolved into the varied myths and legends we encounter in different cultures.

The Babylonian Enuma Elish, for example, is one of the most renowned ancient Mesopotamian creation myths, dating back to the 12th century B.C.E. It begins with the primordial water gods, Apsu and Tiamat, and proceeds through a complex storyline involving divine conflict, the rise and fall of gods, and the eventual creation of humanity from the blood of a defeated god. The Hebrew word *tehom* (תְּהוֹם), "deep," found in Genesis 1:2, is etymologically linked to Tiamat, yet the context is entirely different. While Tiamat is a deity engaged in a cosmic battle, *tehom* is simply a component of the unformed creation, void of any divine personality or mythological conflict.

In *Egyptian mythology*, the creation involves a multitude of deities with the sun god Ra playing a significant role. The world arises from the primordial waters of chaos called *Nun*, and it is through the thoughts and words of Ra that creation takes place. Unlike these mythical deities, the God of Genesis speaks creation into existence (*bara* בָּרָא) with authority and order, not through a process of divine thought or conflict but by the expression of His will.

The *Greek creation narrative* in Hesiod's *Theogony* describes creation in terms of divine progeny and succession, where the gods themselves are subject to a temporal beginning. Contrast this with the Hebrew conception where Jehovah exists outside of time and is the singular uncaused cause of all that exists, not a being born or coming into being as a result of cosmological events.

Similarly, *Norse mythology* unfolds with the story of Ymir, the primeval being whose body parts are used to craft the world, and the ash tree Yggdrasil which supports the universe. Again, the Genesis narrative contains no such anthropomorphic or animistic elements; the heavens and the earth are not fashioned from any pre-existing materials or divine beings but are created *ex nihilo*, out of nothing, by the spoken command of Jehovah.

Hindu cosmology presents a cyclical understanding of the universe, which is eternally recreated and destroyed in vast epochs of time. Genesis, however, describes a linear beginning, where time and creation have a definitive starting point.

As families scattered from Babel, carrying with them the remembrance of creation, their stories became influenced by their developing religious beliefs and worldviews. These stories often elevated elements of the created world (sun, moon, animals, etc.) to divine status, a process known as deification. It stands in stark contrast to the biblical account, where creation is clearly distinct from the Creator, and there is a firm denouncement of idolatry (the worship of created things rather than the Creator).

Moreover, the Hebrew Scriptures meticulously distinguish between God's direct creative acts and his providential guidance of the natural order. For instance, the word *asah* (עָשָׂה), often translated as "made" or "done," implies that Jehovah is both the architect and sustainer of creation, a concept missing in mythological narratives where the gods often seem subject to or part of the cosmic order.

Understanding the ancient mindset reveals a tendency towards *etiological* tales—stories crafted to explain why the world is the way it is. These narratives often include elements of the societies from which they originate, reflecting their customs, values, and fears. In contrast, the Genesis account does not serve an etiological function for Hebrew society; instead, it establishes the sovereignty of

Jehovah, who is above and beyond the cultural and natural world, and whose purposes are not bound by human concerns or limitations.

As a historical record, the Genesis creation account provides a foundation for understanding the nature of God, the purpose of humanity, and the intrinsic order and goodness of the created world. It rejects the notion of the world being borne out of conflict or the body parts of defeated gods, presenting instead a vision of a world created by a divine act of will, purposeful and good. This historical account, free from the mythological embellishments found in other ancient narratives, serves as a bedrock for the theology that underpins the rest of Scripture.

The Babylonian Creation Myth

In the landscape of ancient Near Eastern mythology, the Babylonian creation epic, known as the *Enuma Elish*, occupies a prominent place. It is a tale woven with the themes of chaos, conflict, and the ordering of the cosmos by divine activity. In analyzing the *Enuma Elish*, one must consider the cultural and religious milieu from which it emerged—a milieu steeped in polytheism, divine rivalry, and cosmic warfare.

The *Enuma Elish* begins with the primordial gods Apsu and Tiamat, representing the fresh and salt waters, respectively, who gave birth to a younger generation of gods. As these younger deities grow, they become troublesome to Apsu, prompting his desire to destroy them—a narrative arc driven by generational conflict, a common motif in mythologies where the old order must give way to the new. In stark contrast, the Genesis creation account contains no hint of divine conflict or succession; it is marked by order, intentionality, and harmony. The

225

Hebrew term for create, *bara* (בָּרָא), used exclusively in reference to divine activity, conveys creation by divine decree, not through conflict or combat.

Tiamat, the mother deity who embodies the chaotic waters, becomes vengeful after Apsu's demise. She wages war against the younger gods, leading to her defeat by Marduk, who then creates the world from her split carcass. This violent cosmogony bears no resemblance to the serene and orderly process described in Genesis, where the earth was *tohu va-bohu* (תֹּהוּ וָבֹהוּ), formless and void, and then shaped by the word of Jehovah, not by the dismemberment of deities.

The creation of humanity in the *Enuma Elish* is an afterthought, a byproduct of the gods' desire for relief from labor. Humans are made from the blood of Kingu, a god associated with Tiamat's revolt. This utilitarian view of humanity vastly differs from the dignity and purpose imbued in humanity in Genesis, where humans are created *b'tselem Elohim* (בְּצֶלֶם אֱלֹהִים), in the image of God, and given dominion over the creation, reflecting a profound value placed upon human beings as bearers of the divine image.

Furthermore, the character of Marduk, the hero-god of the *Enuma Elish*, is elevated through his victory over Tiamat and his creative acts. This is a portrayal of a god rising in status among a pantheon, a stark contrast to the biblical God, who needs no elevation as He is eternally sovereign and unrivaled in power and glory. The monotheistic ethos of Genesis sharply diverges from the polytheistic setting of the *Enuma Elish*, emphasizing Jehovah's unique, unchallenged supremacy.

When considering the *Enuma Elish* in the context of the Genesis creation narrative, one can see that any superficial similarities—such as the motif of chaos and order or the presence of waters—dissipate under scrutiny. The themes, characters, and underlying theology of the two accounts are fundamentally different. Genesis presents a monotheistic worldview anchored in the belief in one God who is transcendent yet immanent, while the *Enuma Elish* reflects a polytheistic and mythological worldview where the divine and the mundane are inextricably linked in a pantheon of gods who exhibit very human-like traits and limitations.

In the *Enuma Elish*, the created order reflects the violent and capricious nature of its gods, a universe born from conflict and serving the whims of its creators. In contrast, the Genesis account depicts a universe created with purpose and precision, a reflection of the nature of Jehovah who is orderly, purposeful, and good. Humanity's role within each narrative further amplifies this divergence: whereas the Babylonian account reduces humans to servants of the gods created from the residue of divine battle, the Genesis account elevates humanity to a position of stewardship and communion with Jehovah.

In conclusion, while the *Enuma Elish* and the Genesis creation narrative may arise from the same ancient Near Eastern world, they represent fundamentally distinct conceptions of the divine, humanity, and the world. The biblical account stands unique in its theology, anthropology, and cosmology—asserting a worldview that shaped the course of Judeo-Christian thought, in stark relief against the polytheistic narratives of its time. This divergence underscores the distinctive nature of the Genesis creation narrative, not as myth or legend, but as an account that posits a transcendent order and purpose to the cosmos, defined by the singular, sovereign act of Jehovah.

CHAPTER 12 The Continuation of the Spiritual Gifts?

Gift of Tongues

The gift of tongues, or *glossolalia* as it is known from the Greek γλῶσσα (*glōssa*, meaning "tongue" or "language") and λαλέω (*laleō*, meaning "to speak"), has been a subject of significant interest and debate within Christian circles. This miraculous gift, as recorded in the New Testament, enabled early Christians to speak in languages they had not previously learned. It served as a sign to unbelievers, particularly Jews, and played a crucial role in the spread of the gospel message.

In the nascent Christian community, this phenomenon first appears during the day of Pentecost as described in Acts 2. The Holy Spirit empowered the apostles to speak in various languages, which astonished the multiethnic crowd gathered in Jerusalem. The purpose of this event was twofold: to validate the apostles' divine commission and to facilitate the communication of the gospel across linguistic barriers. The term used for tongues in this context, *heterais glossais* (ἑτέραις γλώσσαις), emphasizes that these were known human languages, not ecstatic utterances.

The apostolic authority to bestow gifts of the Spirit, including tongues, through the laying on of hands was evident in the early church. It is imperative to understand that these gifts were not indiscriminate but were given through apostolic mediation. After the death of the last apostle, John, around 100 C.E., the direct line of this apostolic authority ceased. The historical record from the late second century onward reflects a noticeable absence of the practice of speaking in tongues.

In the first century, the use of tongues was instrumental for the rapid expansion of Christianity. It signified a new covenant and a new pathway to God, distinct from the Old Covenant with Israel. By 33 C.E., the gift of tongues played a pivotal role on the day of Pentecost and subsequently in the life of the early church. As noted by Paul in his first letter to the Corinthians, speaking in tongues was a sign for unbelievers, not believers (1 Corinthians 14:22). This aligns with the overarching purpose of the miraculous gifts: to bear witness to the truth of the gospel and to affirm God's power working through His chosen emissaries.

By the time Christianity had grown to encompass over a million adherents, a significant milestone considering the estimated total population of 150 million in the ancient world, the initial purpose of the gift of tongues had been fulfilled. The message of salvation through Christ had been firmly established and widely disseminated throughout the known world, and the ecclesiastical structure of the Christian church was taking a more defined shape.

The cessation of the gift of tongues corresponded with the establishment of the Christian canon. As the New Testament writings were disseminated, recognized, and read in the congregations, the function of tongues as a revelatory vehicle became obsolete. The written Word of God in the scriptures provided a clear and accessible guide for faith and practice, serving the needs of the growing church and reducing the reliance on direct supernatural manifestations such as tongues.

The resurgence of speaking in tongues in modern times, especially within the Charismatic movement, often lacks the distinguishing characteristics of the biblical gift. Notably, modern instances frequently involve non-linguistic, ecstatic speech, which contrasts with the clear, intelligible languages spoken by the early Christians as recorded in Acts. This contemporary practice does not align with the historical pattern set by the apostolic church nor does it conform to the scriptural guidelines laid out by Paul, who emphasized order, edification, and understanding in the use of spiritual gifts.

In conclusion, the gift of tongues as described in the New Testament was a sign for the foundational period of the church, authenticating the apostles' message and facilitating the spread of the gospel across language barriers. Its purpose was bound to the unique context of the early church's establishment and expansion. As the scriptural canon was completed and the apostolic age concluded, the need for such miraculous gifts diminished. This historical and scriptural context suggests that the continuation of the gift of tongues as originally manifested is not a feature of the post-apostolic church, aligning with the broader biblical principle that miracles were signs accompanying the foundational stages of God's redemptive work in history.

Prophetic Gifts

The *prophetic gifts* refer to the divine enablement given to individuals to receive and proclaim messages from Jehovah, which could concern immediate guidance, future events, or deeper insights into divine truths. In the context of Christian Scripture, these gifts were particularly significant during the foundational era of the church, when the New Testament canon had not yet been formalized.

MIRACLES

In the Old Testament, prophets like Isaiah and Jeremiah received revelations from Jehovah about the future of Israel, the coming Messiah, and the ultimate destiny of humanity. This prophetic gift was not merely about foretelling events but was fundamentally a means for God to communicate His will to His people.

In the New Testament, the Greek word for prophet, *prophētēs* (προφήτης), carries this tradition forward. Prophets are referenced throughout Acts and the Pauline epistles as playing a crucial role in the early church by providing guidance and revelation. For instance, Agabus was a Christian prophet in the first century who predicted a severe famine and the imprisonment of the apostle Paul (Acts 11:28, 21:10-11).

However, as the apostolic era reached its conclusion with the death of the apostle John around 100 C.E., the active presence of the prophetic gifts as seen in the apostolic church appears to have ceased. The close of the first century marked the completion of the New Testament writings, which were subsequently recognized and disseminated as Scripture by the early church. With the establishment of the New Testament canon, there was no longer a need for ongoing prophetic revelations, as the canon itself contained all that was necessary for teaching, reproof, correction, and training in righteousness (2 Timothy 3:16-17).

The cessation of the prophetic gifts aligns with the scriptural depiction that they would not be a permanent fixture within the life of the church. Paul suggests as much in 1 Corinthians 13:8, where he states that prophecies will *fail*, tongues will *cease*, and knowledge will *vanish away*. The Greek term *katargēthēsontai* (καταργηθήσονται), translated as "fail" or "pass away", indicates a cessation of functioning. This cessation was not because of a lack of faith or spirituality among Christians but was a natural progression in God's unfolding plan.

It is essential to recognize that the prophetic gifts were not primarily about predicting the future but were more fundamentally a means by which Jehovah provided guidance to His people. With the completed scriptures, God's people now had a full and sufficient revelation of His will. This special guidance through direct revelation was no longer necessary.

Additionally, the historical record indicates a significant shift in the post-apostolic church's understanding and practice concerning the prophetic gifts. The writings of the early church fathers show an increasing emphasis on the authority of the Scriptures and a corresponding decline in the emphasis on direct prophetic revelation. This is not to say that God ceased to work in history or that He no longer intervened in the lives of believers, but rather that the mode of His working shifted from the miraculous gifts to the guidance provided through His inspired Word.

In conclusion, while the prophetic gifts were instrumental in the establishment and expansion of the early Christian church, their continuation ceased with the death of the last apostle and the completion of the New Testament canon. The transition from a living voice of prophecy to a written Word reflects the progressive revelation of Jehovah's purpose and the sufficiency of the Scriptures as the ultimate authority for the Christian faith and practice. The historical and scriptural evidence thus suggests that the expectation of continuing prophetic gifts in the same manner as the first century is not aligned with the pattern God has set forth in His dealings with His people.

Miraculous Gifts

In the narrative of the Christian Scriptures, miraculous gifts played a vital role in the establishment and expansion of the early church. These gifts, as recorded in the New Testament, included a range of supernatural works— *healings*, *prophecy*, *tongues* (speaking in languages unknown to the speaker), and *interpretation of tongues*, among others. They served as signs of divine approval and as credentials for the apostles and other early church leaders, confirming the message of the Gospel in a world where the written Word of God—the New Testament—was not yet available.

The Purpose of Miraculous Gifts

The initial outpouring of miraculous gifts, particularly evident on the day of Pentecost in 33 C.E., demonstrated Jehovah's power in a tangible form. The apostles were endowed with the *dunamis* (δύναμις), the power to perform signs and wonders, which served as a divine stamp of authenticity on their ministry (Acts 2:22). These signs were instrumental in capturing the attention of a skeptical audience and provided a bridge for the message of salvation to be heard and accepted.

Healings and Signs

The Gospels and Acts are replete with accounts of miraculous healings. For instance, Peter healed a man lame from birth at the temple gate called Beautiful, which not only amazed the onlookers but also provided an opportunity for the Gospel to be proclaimed (Acts 3:1-10). Similarly, Paul's healings in various cities, like the healing of the father of Publius in Malta, are portrayed as signs of God's power working through the apostles (Acts 28:7-9).

233

The Duration of Miraculous Gifts

However, these gifts, while prominent in the early decades of the church's history, were not intended to be permanent. The New Testament itself hints at their eventual cessation. For example, in 1 Corinthians 13:8-10, Paul talks about the time when the *teleion* (τέλειον)—the complete or perfect—comes, the partial will pass away. While interpretations vary, many conservative scholars agree that the "perfect" refers to the completion of the New Testament canon. Once the full revelation of God was available in written form, the need for confirmatory signs diminished.

The Apostolic Foundation

A critical aspect of the miraculous gifts was their association with the apostles. The ability to perform miracles and to bestow gifts of the spirit through the laying on of hands seems to have been uniquely associated with the apostolic office. After the apostle John's death around 100 C.E., there is a notable absence of authoritative claims of such gifts in the historical records of Christianity. The age of the apostles, who were eyewitnesses to Christ's life, death, and resurrection, had passed, and with it, the era of miracles that confirmed their message.

Historical Decline

From the second century C.E. onwards, references to the active presence of miraculous gifts in the life of the church are sparse and often associated with heterodox groups or controversial figures. The patristic writings focus more on the interpretation and application of the established scriptural texts rather than on ongoing supernatural revelations or signs.

The Sufficient Word

By the end of the first century, with the writings of the apostles circulating among the churches, there was a growing sense of the sufficiency of the Scriptures for the faith and practice of the believer. The epistles of Paul, Peter, John, and others were read, shared, and eventually canonized, forming the New Testament. These texts provided the doctrinal foundation, moral instruction, and spiritual encouragement necessary for the church's life and godliness.

Implications for Today

In the contemporary context, the cessation of the miraculous gifts does not equate to a cessation of God's activity in the world. Jehovah is still at work, though His primary means of communication is through the Scriptures. The Bible serves as the complete and final revelation of God's will for humanity. Miracles today are understood not as normative or expected events but as part of the biblical history that points us to the sufficiency of Scripture and the completed work of Christ.

In conclusion, the conservative, scriptural understanding asserts that miraculous gifts were a first-century phenomenon linked to the apostolic witness and the foundational period of the church. With the death of the last apostle and the closure of the biblical canon, the regular occurrence of these gifts ceased. The divine strategy shifted from miraculous signs to the enduring power of the proclaimed Word and the indwelling message of the Gospel, which continue to transform lives. The Bible, complete and powerful, is the believer's ultimate authority, thoroughly equipping the man of God for every good work (2 Timothy 3:16-17). Therefore, while the faith once delivered to the saints is vibrant and alive, the mode through which Jehovah confirms His message has transitioned from the miraculous gifts of the first century to the enduring witness of the Holy Scriptures.

Purpose of Miracles

The biblical narrative unfolds a tapestry of miracles, each acting as a divine signpost signaling significant transitions in Jehovah's dealings with humanity. These supernatural acts were not arbitrary displays of power but served distinct purposes in the unfolding story of God's relationship with His people.

Evidence of Change: Abraham's Call

When Jehovah directed Abraham to leave his country and go to the land of Canaan, it marked the beginning of a distinct people through whom Jehovah would reveal His purposes. The miraculous nature of Abraham's journey and the subsequent promise of descendants, as many as the stars in the sky, signified a monumental shift in how Jehovah was interacting with humanity. This shift is underscored by the extraordinary event of Jehovah passing between the animal halves, an act confirming His covenant with Abraham (Genesis 15:17-18).

Moses and the Exodus

The exodus of the Israelites from Egypt under Moses' leadership is dense with miracles, from the ten plagues, including the *nakat bechorot* (נַכַּת בְּכוֹרוֹת), the striking of the firstborn, to the parting of the Red Sea. Each miracle served a dual purpose: to demonstrate Jehovah's sovereignty over the false gods of Egypt and to signal the establishment of Israel as a nation under His direct rulership. These acts were evidence of the radical change occurring as Jehovah took a slave people and formed them into a nation for His name.

Miracles in Old Testament History

Throughout the Hebrew Scriptures, miracles often coincided with pivotal moments in Israel's history. Elijah's confrontation with the prophets of Baal on Mount Carmel, where Jehovah sent fire from heaven to consume the offering (1 Kings 18:38), was a powerful reaffirmation of His supremacy and a call to repentance. Likewise, the preservation of Daniel in the lion's den (Daniel 6) showcased Jehovah's ability to protect and vindicate His faithful servants.

The Coming of the Messiah

The New Testament opens with the miracle of the virgin birth of Jesus, an event that announced the advent of the Messiah. Jesus's ministry was characterized by miracles, such as the healing of the sick, raising the dead, and feeding thousands with just a few loaves of bread and fish. These miracles were signs of the presence of God's Kingdom and served as evidence of Jesus' authority and identity as the promised Messiah. For example, when John the Baptist sent messengers to inquire if Jesus was the one to come, Jesus referred to His miraculous works as the evidence for John to consider (Luke 7:22).

Miracles as Harbingers of New Covenants

The miracles in the Bible often accompanied the establishment of new covenants. Just as the signs and wonders in Egypt and at Sinai were tied to the Mosaic Covenant, the miracles of Jesus and the apostles were linked with the New Covenant. This New Covenant provided a new way to approach Jehovah through Christ's sacrificial death and resurrection, as shown by the tearing of the temple veil at Jesus's death (Matthew 27:51).

The Great Tribulation and Armageddon

The New Testament foretells a time of great tribulation and the battle of Armageddon as critical events in God's plan. The Book of Revelation, written by John, contains symbolic visions of this period, some of which include miraculous elements. These future miracles are depicted as acts of divine judgment and deliverance, signifying the final stages of Jehovah's purpose and the establishment of His Kingdom's rule on earth.

Miracles and the Canon

With the completion of the New Testament canon, a new epoch commenced in which the recorded Word provided the guide for faith and practice. The miracles in the early church, as recorded by the apostles, authenticated their message and ministry. Once the apostolic age concluded with John's death around 100 C.E., the primary role of miracles as evidentiary support for new revelation also concluded.

Conclusion on the Purpose of Miracles

In sum, the Bible presents miracles as signs accompanying and authenticating God's major acts of revelation and transition. From Abraham to Moses, from the prophets to the Messiah, miracles served as divine endorsements of God's messengers and milestones in His salvific history with humankind. Post-apostolic claims to miraculous gifts tend to lack the direct association with divine revelation that characterized the biblical miracles. The scriptural record, now complete, serves as Jehovah's final and sufficient revelation, not necessitating further authentication by miracles. The miracles of the Bible, therefore, are foundational rather than normative for subsequent generations, pointing us to the enduring truth of God's Word and His ultimate revelation in Jesus Christ.

APPENDIX Saints in Christian Belief

Definition and Biblical Context

In Christianity, particularly from a biblical perspective, saints (holy ones preferred rendering, USV) are individuals set apart by God, living lives in service to Him and others. The term "saint" originates from the Greek word "hagios," meaning "holy" or "set apart." Although Roman Catholic tradition reserves the title of "saint" for those canonized after death, recognized for extraordinary holiness, and considered as intercessors in heaven, the Bible provides a broader application.

Saints on Earth According to Scripture

The Bible does indeed mention saints in heaven, with Jehovah described as the ultimate Holy One and Jesus Christ as the Holy One of God, both on earth and in heaven. Similarly, angels are referred to as holy. However, the term "saints" also applies to faithful individuals on earth, as evidenced by numerous scriptural passages.

For instance, in Acts 9:32, 36-41, "saints" refers to living followers of Christ in Lydda. These saints were not in heaven but were among the congregation of believers on earth. Similarly, in 2 Corinthians 1:1 and 13:12, Paul addresses the Corinthian Christians, calling them saints, indicating their holy status due to their dedication and cleansing by Christ's sacrifice.

The Role of "Saints" in Intercession

As for the practice of praying to saints as intercessors, the biblical model centers prayer on God the Father, through Jesus Christ. Jesus taught His disciples to pray to "Our Father in heaven," emphasizing a direct relationship with God (Matthew 6:9). He also stated that He is the only way to the Father and the sole mediator (John 14:6, 14). The apostle Paul affirms that Jesus is our intercessor before God (Romans 8:34; Hebrews 7:25).

Praying for Saints, Not to Saints

Ephesians 6:18, 19 encourages believers to pray for all saints, not to them. This indicates the early Christian practice of intercessory prayer among living believers, supporting and strengthening each other in their faith journey. Romans 15:30 illustrates this, as Paul requests prayers for himself from other saints, demonstrating a mutual relationship of prayerful support rather than a hierarchical one based on posthumous status.

The biblical evidence points to the use of the term "saints" as applicable to all who are dedicated to God, whether on earth or in heaven. Scripture directs believers to approach God directly through Jesus Christ and not through other intermediaries. This practice reflects the personal and communal aspects of Christian prayer and underscores the immediate access to God afforded by Christ's mediating role.

Saints and Their Veneration

What is the Stance on Relics and Images?

The veneration of relics and images, as recognized by sources such as the *New Catholic Encyclopedia*, does not find a strong foothold in biblical tradition. The practices surrounding relics, in particular, have no clear endorsement from the Scriptures. For example, Moses, a significant figure in the faith, was buried by God in an undisclosed location to prevent the very possibility of his grave becoming a site of veneration (Deuteronomy 34:5, 6). Even the archangel Michael contended with the Devil over Moses' body, potentially to thwart any idolatrous outcomes (Jude 9). The implication here is that God's intention was to avoid human fixation on physical remains, which could detract from worship directed towards Him alone.

Why the Halo in Depictions of Saints?

As to why traditional depictions of "saints" often include halos, the historical origin is telling. According to the *New Catholic Encyclopedia* and the *New Encyclopædia Britannica*, the halo has its roots in pre-Christian art, symbolizing figures from paganism. Early Christian art was initially hesitant to adopt such symbolism due to its association with pagan deities. However, by the 6th century, the halo had become a common feature in Christian iconography, not only for Christ but also for Mary and other saints—despite its non-Christian origins.

Christianity's Position on Pagan Elements

Integrating pagan elements into Christian worship raises important questions. The Apostle Paul's words in 2

Corinthians 6:14-18 emphatically call for a separation from practices that are not of faith in Christ. Drawing from this scriptural standpoint, the merging of Christian belief with pagan symbolism is cautioned against, encouraging a pure form of worship devoid of idolatrous influences.

Are All Believers Sinless Saints?

The New Testament does indeed describe the early Christian community as saints, referring to those who had been forgiven and set apart for God's purposes (1 Corinthians 1:2; Acts 26:18). However, these individuals did not claim sinlessness. The inherited imperfection from Adam meant that even the apostles, including Paul, acknowledged an ongoing struggle with sin (Romans 7:21-25). The Apostle John stated it unequivocally: claiming sinlessness is self-deception, not a reflection of the truth within us (1 John 1:8). Therefore, the term "saint" in the biblical context does not equate to being without sin while in the flesh.

Bibliography

Anders, M., & Lawson, S. (2004). *Holman Old Testament Commentary - Psalms: 11.* Grand Rapids: B&H Publishing.

Andrews, E. D. (2015). *EVIDENCE THAT YOU ARE TRULY CHRISTIAN: Keep Testing Yourselves to See If You Are In the Faith - Keep Examining Yourselves.* Cambridge, OH: Christian Publishing House.

Andrews, E. D. (2016). *INTERPRETING THE BIBLE: Introduction to Biblical Hermeneutics.* Cambridge, OH: Christian Publishing House.

Andrews, E. D. (2016). *THE CHRISTIAN APOLOGIST: Always Being Prepared to Make a Defense [Second Edition].* Cambridge, OH: Christian Publishing House.

Andrews, E. D. (2016). *YOUR GUIDE FOR DEFENDING THE BIBLE: Self-Education of the Bible Made Easy.* Cambridge, OH: Christian Publishing House.

Andrews, E. D. (2017). *HOW TO STUDY YOUR BIBLE: Rightly Handling the Word of God.* Cambridge, OH: Christian Publishing House.

Andrews, E. D. (2017). *HUMAN IMPERFECTION: While We Were Sinners Christ Died For Us.* Cambridge, OH: Christian Ppublishing House.

Andrews, E. D. (2017). *THE OUTSIDER: Coming-of-Age In This Moment.* Cambridge, OH: Christian Publishing House.

Andrews, E. D. (2017). *TURN OLD HABITS INTO NEW HABITS: Why and How the Bible Makes a*

Difference. Cambridge, OH: Christian Publishing House.

Andrews, E. D. (2018). *LET GOD USE YOU TO SOLVE YOUR PROBLEMS: GOD Will Instruct You and Teach You In the Way You Should Go.* Cambridge, OH: Christian Publishing House.

Andrews, E. D. (2018). *WHY ME?: When Bad Things Happen to Good People.* Cambridge, OH: Christian Publishing House.

Andrews, E. D. (2019). *SATAN: Know Your Enemy.* Cambridge, OH: Christian Publishing House.

Andrews, E. D. (2023). *BIBLICAL EXEGESIS: Biblical Criticism on Trial.* Cambridge, OH: Christian Publishing House.

Andrews, E. D. (2023). *CHRISTIAN APOLOGETICS: Answering the Tough Questions: Evidence and Reason in Defense of the Faith.* Cambridge, Ohio: Christian Publishing House.

Andrews, E. D. (2023). *FAITHFUL MINDS: A Biblical and Cognitive Behavioral Therapy Approach to Mental Health and Wellness.* Cambridge, OH: Christian Publishing House.

Andrews, E. D. (2023). *HOW WE GOT THE BIBLE.* Cambridge, OH: Christian Publishing House.

Andrews, E. D. (2023). *LIFE DOES HAVE A PURPOSE: Discovering and Living Your Ultimate Purpose.* Cambridge, OH: Christian Publishing House.

Andrews, E. D. (2023). *MERE CHRISTIANITY REIMAGINED: Rediscovering the Faith for the 21st Century.* Cambridge, OH: Christian Publishing House.

Andrews, E. D. (2023). *THE BIBLE AS HISTORY: A Historical Journey Through the Bible.* Cambridge, Ohio: Christian Publishing House.

Andrews, E. D. (2023). *THE BIBLE ON TRIAL: Examining the Evidence for Being Inspired, Inerrant, Authentic, and True.* Cambridge, Ohio: Christian Publishing House.

Andrews, E. D. (2023). *THE BOOK OF PROVERBS Chapters 1-15: CPH Old Testament Commentary: Volume 17.* Cambridge, OH: Christian Publishing House.

Andrews, E. D. (2023). *THE BOOK OF PROVERBS Chapters 16-23: CPH Old Testament Commentary: Volume 18.* Cambridge, OH: Christian Publishing House.

Andrews, E. D. (2023). *THE EXPOSITORY DICTIONARY: A Companion Study Tool to the Updated American Standard Version.* Cambridge, OH: Christian Publishing House.

Andrews, E. D. (2023). *UNSHAKABLE BELIEFS: Strategies for Strengthening and Defending Your Faith.* Cambridge, OH: Christian Publishing House.

Andrews, E. D., & Marshall, T. F. (2023). *PAUL'S LETTER TO THE EPHESIANS: CPH New Testament Commentary.* Cambridge, OH: Christian Publishing House.

Andrews, E. D., & Torrey, R. A. (2016). *Christian Living: How to Succeed in the Christian Life.* Cambridge, OH: Christian Publishing House.

Bercot, D. W. (1998). *A Dictionary of Early Christian Beliefs.* Peabody: Hendrickson.

Brand, C., Draper, C., & Archie, E. (2003). *Holman Illustrated Bible Dictionary: Revised, Updated and Expanded.* Nashville, TN: Holman.

Bromiley, G. W. (1986). *The International Standard Bible Encyclopedia (Vol. 1-4).* Grand Rapids, MI: William B. Eerdmans Publishing Co.

Campbell, A. (1850). *The Christian System (6th ed.;.* Cincinnati: Standard.

Elwell, W. A. (1988). *Baker Encyclopedia of the Bible.* Grand Rapids: Baker Book House.

Elwell, W. A. (2001). *Evangelical Dictionary of Theology (Second Edition).* Grand Rapids: Baker Academic.

Elwell, W. A., & Comfort, P. W. (2001). *Tyndale Bible Dictionary.* Wheaton, Ill: Tyndale House Publishers.

Enns, P. P. (1997). *The Moody Handbook of Theology.* Chicago: Moody Press.

Erickson, M. J. (1992). *Introducing Christian Doctrine.* Grand Rapids: Baker Book Hous.

Erickson, M. J. (1998). *Christian Theology.* Grand Rapids, MI: Baker Academic.

Green, J. B., McKnight, S., & Marshall, H. (1992). *Dictionary of Jesus and the Gospels.* Downers Grove, IL: InterVarsity Press.

Gruden, W. (2011). *Are Miraculous Gifts for Today?: 4 Views (Counterpoints: Bible and Theology).* Grand Rapids: Zondervan.

Hoerth, A. (1998). *Archaeology and the Old Testament.* Grand Rapids: Baker.

Kistemaker, S. J., & Hendriksen, W. (1953–2001). *Exposition of the First Epistle to the Corinthians, vol. 18, New Testament Commentary.* Grand Rapids, MI: Baker Book House.

Kittel, G., Friedrich, G., & Bromiley, G. W. (1995, c1985). *Theological Dictionary of the New Testament.* Grand Rapids: Eerdmans.

Marshall, T. F., & Andrews, E. D. (2022). *PAUL'S LETTER TO THE PHILIPPIANS: An Apologetic and Background Exposition of the Holy Scriptures.* Cambridge, Ohio: Christian publishing House.

Microsoft. (1998-2010). *Encarta ® World English Dictionary.* Redmond: Microsoft Corporation. Retrieved April 10, 2010, from http://encarta.msn.com/encnet/features/dictionary/dictionaryhome.aspx

Mirriam-Webster, I. (2003). *Mirriam-Webster's Collegiate Dictionary. Eleventh Edition.* Springfield: Mirriam-Webster, Inc.

Mounce, W. D. (2006). *Mounce's Complete Expository Dictionary of Old & New Testament Words.* Grand Rapids, MI: Zondervan.

Stein, R. H. (1994). *A Basic Guide to Interpreting the Bible: Playing by the Rules.* Grand Rapids: Baker Books.

Sweeney, Z. T. (2005). *The Spirit and the Word (: , n.d.), 121–26.* Nashville: Gospel Advocate.

Towns, E. L. (2002). *Theology for Today.* Belmont: Wadsworth Group.

Vine, W. E. (1996). *Vine's Expository Dictionary of Old and New Testament Words.* Nashville: Thomas Nelson.

Wood, D. R. (1996). *New Bible Dictionary (Third Edition).* Downers Grove: InterVarsity Press.

Zodhiates, S. (2000, c1992, c1993). *The Complete Word Study Dictionary: New Testament.* Chattanooga: AMG Publishers.